INTRODUCTION TO RATIO ANALYSIS

Trupti Gadgil

Disclaimer:

Every effort is made to give credit to the sources where it is due. There is no intent to plagiarize. However, if inadvertently, the author has forgotten to give due credit, the author is most willing to rectify the mistake without hesitation.

Every effort is made to cover most important ratios. However, due to the sheer volume of the ratios, the author expresses regret that some ratios may be inadvertently missed. The author is deeply sorry for the lapse, if any.

Dedicated to my great-grandparents, Mr. Dhananjay Ramchandra Gadgil and Mrs. Pramila Dhananjay Gadgil

INDEX

ACKNOWLEDGEMENTS

I am indebted to my great-grandparents, Mr. D.R. Gadgil and Mrs. P.D. Gadgil for being my inspiration.

I am thankful to my mother, Mrs. Sheela D. Gadgil and my sister Ms. Preeti D. Gadgil for the unconditional and constant support they have provided me.

I am thankful to Om and Siddhi, two beautiful children who shower me with unconditional love.

I am thankful to Mr. Viraj Shah for the help and motivation to write on the subject matter.

INTRODUCTION

Everybody wants to make money. Business is established to earn a profit. Ordinary people with limited incomes also want to increase the amount of money and wealth they have. If businesses don't earn a reward on their investments, known as a profit, they lose confidence of the stakeholders, lose market value and/or shut down. So, earning money is the primary objective of any investment activity. To this end, even banks lend to earn a profit, stock market exists so that share can earn dividends and capital appreciation and businesses earn a profit on their investment. But how do we analyze how much return we have received on our investment? And more importantly, which investment do we make in order to generate a return or profit on the investments? We all realize that resources especially money are limited and the investment opportunities may be many. Thus, a wise choice has to be made.

The stock market is made up of a number of companies whose shares are listed on the stock exchange and these shares are traded on a daily basis. Investors always want to know which stock or share to invest in. It is a well known fact the fortunes of many have been made and lost in the share market. There are many successful investors who swear by a formula that they have come up with. The unsuccessful investors will swear that no such formula exists. It is but obvious to all of us that we all need some kind of tool that is needed to analyze whether the stock that we want to invest in would provide us with benefits in the form of either dividends or capital appreciation. The stock market is filled with examples of how word of mouth publicity has led to buying of certain stocks and how the investors have lost their life savings as a result. Therefore, some amount of analysis of a script or stock is essential in order to ensure that such consequences do not ensue to us.

Besides investing in the stock market, there are investors who want to invest in companies to grow with the companies, not just for the short term trading in equity. These investors will invest capital in the company and share in profits. There are also mergers and acquisitions that happen and they affect the organization as well as the share price of the company. Venture Capitalists also invest in companies in order to make the best of a new opportunity. There are various times, especially during Mergers and Acquisitions that requires companies to be valued. Valuation of a company also has to be done using various methods and formulae. Valuation of companies is done in order to analyze whether the merger would be a good strategic fit.

Besides investors, the banking community is also interested in the companies it deals with. Loans and advances made by banks to companies are based on the financial position of the companies that are being dealt with. Whether a loan would be paid back to the bank would be decided by the financials of the company that are analyzed by the bank. New projects of companies require investment and banks play a crucial part in this. Again, importers and exporters require bank guarantees to perform their international obligations. Banks are therefore extremely interested in the performance of the corporations that they deal with.

There are various techniques available to the investors. The two most common are Technical Analysis and Fundamental Analysis. The methods are vastly different. Technical Analysis believes that past behavior is an indicator of future behavior. It believes that each stock follows a particular pattern and that this pattern will continue in the future and based on this, buy or sell signals are predicted. However, Technical Analysis does not take into consideration the fundamentals of the company that is being analyzed. The market as a whole runs in trends and these trends affect the share price of an organization as well. In a bullish trend, the prices of shares tend to take an upturn whereas the opposite is true in a bearish market. It is this absence of analysis of fundamental facts of an organization that makes Technical Analysis subject to criticism. Another criticism leveled at Technical Analysis is that the buy or sell signal is given after a trend is breached, which means that stock has already started with another trend and some amount of profit is minimized or loss is incurred before action is taken due to the delay in the giving of the signal. Another criticism is that Technical Analysis does not take into consideration the fact that the share price is affected by rumors or noise in the market, leading to an incorrect analysis of the script. On the positive side, Technical Analysis has predicted the rise and fall of certain scripts extremely accurately and much depends on the skill and study of the analyst.

Fundamental Analysis takes a view that is somewhat contrary to Technical Analysis. The concentration of Fundamental Analysis is on the fundamentals of the company in order to analyze whether an investment in the stock should be made, or the stock should be held or sold. The Balance Sheet, The Profit and Loss Account, The Cash Flow Statement, are all important statements that are analyzed in order to make a decision. Various ratios are calculated and the industry in which the company operates is also taken into consideration. The ratios of the company could be compared with the ratios of the previous years, the ratios could be compared with those of its nearest competitors as well as the industry in which it operates as well as the sector as a whole. A full analysis of the company's performance is possible as a result and the market performance can be compared in light of this analysis and a well informed, well rounded decision can be taken by the investors. It is Fundamental Analysis that bankers, investment bankers, venture capitalists as well as valuation analysts are interested in. Fundamental Analysis helps not only these investors but the public at large in making key investment decisions investments. Ratio Analysis is a part of Fundamental Analysis.

WHAT IS RATIO ANALYSIS

According to the Accountant's Handbook by Wixon, Kell and Bedford, "A Ratio is an expression of the quantitative relationship between two numbers".

Since a ratio is used to express relationship between numbers, Ratio Analysis is also used to define a relationship between two numbers from the Balance Sheet as well as the Profit and Loss Account (Income Statement) in quantitative terms that can be used to arrive at a conclusion based on the intention of the user.

Campbell R. Harvey defines Ratio Analysis as, "A way of expressing relationships between a firm's accounting numbers and their trends over time that analysts use to establish values and evaluate risks."

Farlex Financial Dictionary defines Ratio Analysis as, "The study of the significance of financial ratios for a company. Ratio analysis is very important in fundamental analysis, which investigates the financial health of companies. An example of ratio analysis is the comparison of price-earnings ratios of different companies. This helps analysts determine which companies' share prices properly reflect their performances and therefore what investments are most likely to be the most profitable."

Batty J. Management Accounting defines Ratio Analysis as, "Ratio can assist management in its basic functions of forecasting, planning coordination, control and communication".

Investopedia.com defines Ratio Analysis as, "Quantitative analysis of information contained in a company's financial statements. Ratio analysis is based on line items in financial statements like the balance sheet, income statement and cash flow statement; the ratios of one item – or a combination of items - to another item or combination are then calculated. Ratio analysis is used to evaluate various aspects of a company's operating and financial performance such as its efficiency, liquidity, profitability and solvency. The trend of these ratios over time is studied to check whether they are improving or deteriorating. Ratios are also compared across different companies in the same sector to see how they stack up, and to get an idea of comparative valuations. Ratio analysis is a cornerstone of fundamental analysis."

Readyratios.com defines Ratio Analysis as, "Ratio analysis is a tool brought into play by individuals to carry out an evaluative analysis of information in the financial statements of a company. These ratios are calculated from current year figures and then compared to past years, other companies, the industry, and also the company to assess the performance of the company. Besides, ratio analysis is used predominantly by proponents of financial analysis."

Businessdictionary.com defines Ratio Analysis as, "Single most important technique of financial analysis in which quantities are converted into ratios for meaningful comparisons, with past ratios and ratios of other firms in the same or different industries. Ratio analysis determines trends and exposes strengths or weaknesses of a firm."

Ratio Analysis is a tool used in Fundamental Analysis. Ratio Analysis uses analysis of Financial Statements in order to get an idea about the financial performance of an organization. Ratio Analysis can be used by anyone as the information needed to conduct Ratio Analysis is readily available in the form of financial statements. Ratio Analysis can be safely used as a way to ascertain the financial performance of an organization and identify areas where further information or analysis is required.

A ratio is used to express a relationship between two or more numbers. These numbers can both be from the Balance Sheet or the Profit and Loss Account (Income Statement) or one number can be from the Balance Sheet and the other can be from the Profit and Loss Account (Income Statement). As long a relationship between two numbers can be established, a ratio can be meaningful.

For a ratio to be meaningful, the two numbers being compared must have some relationship to each other such that when a comparison is made, the resulting ratio or number must be able to give an indication as to the performance of an organization and help the person conducting the analysis to draw inferences from it in order to arrive at a conclusion based on the point of view from which the analysis is being conducted.

A ratio can be expressed as a percentage (where a number is expressed in terms of a hundredth), a rate (so many times where a figure is so many times when compared to another figure) or as a pure or simple ratio (where one number is divided by another number).

Ratio Analysis can be used to compare the performance of an organization with its own performance over a period of time by comparing ratios over time in order to identify whether performance of different areas in the organization have improved or deteriorated over a period of time. Ratio Analysis can also be used to compare the performance of an organization with competitors within the industry and sector. Thus, Ratio Analysis can also be used for benchmarking purposes by comparing ratios with the best in industry as well as industry and sector average.

There are various kinds of ratios like, Liquidity Ratios, Asset Ratios, Profitability Ratios, and Operational Ratios etc. Different ratios matter to different sets of people. Creditors may be more interested in Liquidity Ratios while shareholders may be more interested in Profitability ratios and so on. However, placing excessive reliance on a single ratio may lead to nothing but taken together, they give an idea about the financial stability and profitability of a firm or organization. A single ratio by itself means not much. It needs to be taken into consideration with other ratios. A single ratio will reveal only one aspect of the company's financials. It has to be noted that just one dimensional approach will cause a lop sided view whereas the combination of all ratios gives an overall balanced perspective of the financial stability and profitability of the firm or organization.

REFERENCES:

1)http://www.businessdictionary.com/definition/ratio-analysis.html#ixzz2vd1AgtyZ
2)http://www.readyratios.com/reference/analysis/ratio_analysis.html
3)http://financial-dictionary.thefreedictionary.com/Ratio+Analysis
4)http://www.investopedia.com/terms/r/ratioanalysis.asp
5)http://www.allprojectreports.com/MBA-Projects/Finance-Project-Report/ratio-analysis/ratio-analysis-advantage-limitations-classification-financial-ratio-analysis.htm

LIQUIDITY RATIOS

The first types of ratios that we consider are the Liquidity Ratios. Liquidity Ratios are those ratios that help determine whether or not the company is able to meet its short term obligations. Liquidity Ratios help calculate the ease with which Current Assets can be converted into cash. Thus Liquidity Ratios help understand the liquidity of the Current Assets. Liquidity Ratios help analyze whether the Working Capital required to conduct a business is adequate or whether outside sources of finance would be required as well as the efficiency in the use of Working Capital. Liquidity Ratios help the long term creditors as well as the shareholders to determine whether interest would be repaid on debt as well as dividends would be paid to the shareholders.

Liquidity Ratios are calculated by dividing current assets that include cash and cash equivalents by current liabilities as well as short term borrowings. The cash cycle of a company is important to the company. Due to an understanding of the cash cycle the concept of liquidity ratios gets understood better.

The Cash Cycle includes buying of raw material, converting raw material into finished goods. These finished goods form inventory that is sold on cash basis or on credit. When goods or services are sold on credit, debtors are given time to pay. Unless debtors pay their dues, creditors for raw materials and other services cannot be paid. Liquidity ratios try to measure the short term assets as well as the short term liabilities of the organization and try to establish whether there is a balance between the two.

There are various types of Liquidity Ratios. The two most basic and the most common are Net Working Capital, Current Ratio and Quick Ratio. Other ratios amongst others that are included in Liquidity Ratios are Cash Ratio, Cash Flow Ratio and Working Capital Ratio.

Net Working Capital:

It is calculated as follows:

Current Assets – Current Liabilities

Current Assets are assets that can be converted into cash or consumed or sold within a short period of time (usually the longer period between a year or an operating cycle). Thus, liquidity ratios generally give an idea about the ability of an organization to carry out its operations in the short run.

Current Assets include Cash and Cash Equivalents, Accounts Receivable, Prepaid Items, Inventory, Marketable Securities.

Current Liabilities are obligations of an organization that have to be settled at the earliest (usually with a year or within an operating cycle, whichever is longer).

Current Liabilities include Accounts Payable, Notes Payable, Taxes Payable, Wages and Salaries Payable, Unearned Revenues, Other items payable.

The liquidity of the Current Liabilities refers to the ability of an organization to raise funds with ease in the form of debt or new structured funds through either convertible funds or callable funds or puttable funds etc. The ability of an organization to raise funds in the financial markets is generally dependant on the size of the organization, reputation of the organization, capital structure and leverage of the organization as well as the creditworthiness of the organization. In order to raise money in an adverse situation, liquidity of assets as well as liquidity of liabilities is essential.

Net Working Capital gives an indication as to the ability of an organization to repay all its Current Liabilities. Net Working Capital gives an idea as to whether the Current Assets are enough to fulfill all the obligations towards the Current Liabilities or whether the organization will have to borrow money to repay the Current Liabilities. In case the Current Assets tend to fall short of the ability to repay Current Liabilities over a period of time. It indicates liquidity issues as well as solvency issues.

If the Working Capital is a positive figure, it indicates that Current Assets are greater than Current Liabilities and hence current obligations can be fulfilled. Increase in Working Capital could be the result of many factors such as cash received from issue of additional shares or debentures, increase in Operating Profits and sale of Non Current Assets or decrease in Current Liabilities.

On the other hand, if the Working Capital is a negative figure, it indicates that Current Assets are lesser than Current Liabilities and hence current obligations cannot be fully fulfilled implying a need to borrow in order to fulfill current obligations. Most organizations at some point in their life cycle go through such short phases. However, if the situation persists over a period of time, it could lead to default and even insolvency. However, a decrease in Working Capital is to be interpreted carefully as it is possible that inspite of a decrease in Working Capital, the current financial position may be strong.

Current Ratio:

The Current Ratio is most widely used to measure liquidity. It is very widely used by creditors especially short term creditors.

Current Ratio is calculated as follows:

Current Assets

Current Liabilities

Current ratio measures the relationship of assets available to pay off current liabilities as a percentage. Net Working Capital would express this in term of a dollar amount. The ideal Current Ratio is 2:1, at least theoretically. A higher Current Ratio could indicate over capitalization and under trading. A lower Current Ratio usually means that there are liquidity issues and that the Current Assets may not be sufficient to pay off Current Liabilities. A lower Current Ratio could indicate under capitalization and over trading. If the Current Ratio is low over a period of time, it could even be indicative of solvency issues. On the other hand, if the Current Ratio is significantly high, assets may be lying idle instead of being used for productive purposes.

However, the Current Ratio is generally proportionate to the operating (cash) cycle. A lower current ratio would be tolerable for a short operating cycle whereas a long operating cycle would usually require a larger current ratio as it is these Current Assets that are required to pay off the Current Liabilities. A short operating cycle would imply that the assets can be converted into cash at a faster rate. A long operating cycle would mean it takes longer for assets to be converted into cash.

The Working Capital Management policy affects the Current Ratio significantly. Any organization wants Working Capital to be kept to a minimum so as to make investments for profit. But this has to be balanced against the risk of not meeting debts and subsequent insolvency. An aggressive financing policy (the willingness to keep lower working capital and assuming the risk of insolvency) means that the Current Ratio would be lower. A conservative financing policy (a higher working capital and lower willingness to assume the risk of insolvency) means a higher Current Ratio.

The Current Ratio must be analyzed further to check for the strength of the ratio. The constituents of the Current Assets must be analyzed further to measure the strength of the Current Ratio. The Accounts Receivable and Inventory have to be looked at closely. Just a high Current Ratio is not enough. Accounts Receivable has Bad Debts as not all debtors pay on time. Some debtors do not pay at all. So, the quality of the debtors must be taken into consideration. For this, the Receivables Turnover Ratio can be calculated to analyze the strength of the Current Ratio. A low Receivables Turnover Ratio means that Receivables are not being converted to Cash rapidly. In case prepaid expenses form a high portion of Current Assets, the Current Ratio is overstated as Prepaid Expenses cannot be converted into cash.

The quality of the Inventory must also be taken into consideration. The Quickness with which Inventory can be converted into cash must also be taken into consideration. Another ratio, the Inventory Turnover Ratio can be calculated in this respect to further analyze the Current Assets Ratio. A low Inventory Turnover Ratio means that inventory is not being converted to cash at a fast rate. If both these ratios are low, it indicates that there is a greater need to have a high amount of Cash and Cash Equivalents in the Current Assets.

Method used for calculation of Inventory also affects the Current Ratio. Use of the LIFO (Last In First Out Method) has the effect of reduction in the amount of Inventory (The latest and higher price (in line with the principle that inflation increases the prices of goods over time) will be included in the Cost of Goods Sold and hence the value of Inventory will be lower.

Similarly when FIFO(First In First Out) method is used for the calculation of Inventory, the value of inventory will increase ((he previous and lower price (in line with the principle that inflation increases the prices of goods over time and the past prices will be lower) will be included in the Cost of Goods Sold and hence the value of Inventory will be higher.

Including Inventories in the Current Ratio will raise the question of the accounting value of the Inventories (whatever method of Inventory Valuation is used) as opposed to the economic value of the Inventories. Any organization is subject to business cycles. During a downturn, Inventories will build up. Even though the market price of the Inventory may not fall, less Inventory may be sold than usual leading to a build up of Inventory. Inspite of the Inventory being carried in the Balance Sheet as an asset. It is difficult to sell the Inventory and convert it into cash in order to mkeet obligations. On the other hand, in case of an up turn, since Inventory is being sold at a fast rate, the Inventory is being converted to Cash at a faster rate and hence less Inventory is being carried in the Balance Sheet as an asset.

The Current Ratio is not without its limitations. The Current Ratio only measures the state of finances if the Cash flow was to come to a complete halt. In such a scenario, the Current Assets would be used to pay off the Current Liabilities. This is contrary to the presumption in accountancy of a going concern principle. To answer the question of liquidity on a going concern basis, Cash Flows can be used. But this does not negate the fact that the Current Ratio is easy to calculate and is simple to understand. The data used in it is also easily available.

Furthermore, the Current Ratio cannot give an idea about the future cash flows and future liquidity of an organization. For example, In case Accounts Receivables forms a high percentage of Current Assets, the expectation is that upon repayment, these Receivables with convert into cash. But there is always a possibility of default by any of the Accounts Receivables. It is also possible that receipt of money from debtors may be delayed. The liquidity of an organization can therefore be affected.

The Current Ratio also does not take into consideration the timing of cash flows. An example would be that a payment to a creditor might be due earlier than the time it might take for inventory to convert into cash. In such a situation, if the value of Inventory in the Current Assets is higher than Cash and Cash Equivalents, there might be a temporary cash crunch.

The Current Ratio is also very susceptible to window dressing or creative accounting where a ratio can be manipulated by increase or decrease of Current Assets and Current Liabilities.

Quick Ratio:

Due to the limitations of the Current Ratio, this ratio is calculated. This ratio is narrower in scope than the Current Ratio. The Quick Ratio is calculated as follows:

$$\frac{\text{Current Assets} - \text{Inventory}}{\text{Current Liabilities}}$$

It is also written as

$$\frac{\text{Cash} + \text{Marketable Securities} + \text{Net Accounts Receivable}}{\text{Current Liabilities}}$$

As well as

$$\frac{\text{Cash} + \text{Cash Equivalents} + \text{Net Receivables} + \text{Short-Term Securities Owned}}{\text{Current Liabilities}}$$

This ratio is also known as the Acid test ratio as this ratio does not include Inventory in the calculation of the Assets. The ideal Quick ratio is said to be 1:1. It is generally observed that if the Quick Ratio is less than 1:1, inventory or other assets are greater relied on in Current Assets as compared to other Current Assets for repayment of debt. Similarly, it is also observed that if the Quick Ratio is greater than 1:1, there is a greater ability to repay debt through Cash and Cash Equivalents and Marketable Securities. The Quick Ratio can range from either extremely high to extremely low.

The flow of future cash flows that are based on Inventory are uncertain as there is no guarantee when Inventory would be able to be converted to Cash. Furthermore, if Inventory is used to pay Current Liabilities, the future cash flows of the organization would halt.

Prepaid Expenses and Deferred Taxes are also not included in the Quick Assets for calculation of the Quick Ratio. The reason is that they cannot be used to pay off Current Liabilities. Prepaid Expenses are merely payments made in advance towards certain expenses such as Rent paid in Advance or Insurance paid in Advance. Deferred Taxes cannot be used to pay Current Liabilities and they would have to be paid in future periods.

Although Inventory is not included, Accounts Receivable is included in the calculation of Quick Assets. The reason is that while Inventory is two steps away from cash, Accounts Receivable is just one step away from cash. Furthermore, Receivables are capable of being factored.

An advantage of this method is that Inventory is not included and hence the effect of the method used for the calculation of Inventory is avoided. The problem of Inventory valuation is avoided.

Cash Ratio:

The Cash Ratio can be said to be a part of the Current Ratio but it is much narrower. It is even narrower in scope than the Quick Ratio. The Cash Ratio is calculated as follows:

$$\frac{Cash + Cash\ Equivalents + Short\text{-}Term\ Securities\ Owned}{Current\ Liabilities}$$

Cash Ratio is a ratio that only measures liquid cash to Current Liabilities. Cash Equivalents are extremely liquid with extremely short maturities. They have maturities up to 90 days only. Cash Equivalents are investments made with excess cash for extremely small maturities. They can be converted into liquid cash as and when needed. Short term securities are tradable securities. They are available at hand and can be sold in the market as and when necessary, usually within a year or depending on the operating cycle, whichever is longer. In practice, the Cash Ratio is not used very often in analyzing the financial statements.

An ideal Cash Ratio could be 1:2. A low Cash Ratio could indicate liquidity issues implying a need to borrow and if the Cash Ratio is consistently low over a period of time, it could imply default and even insolvency. A high Cash Ratio on the other hand may imply that the organization is not using its cash resources wisely and that there is idle cash that could be used for other productive purposes.

In practice, an organization may not always have cash and cash equivalents in hand at all times. It may be very difficult to maintain high levels of cash as idle cash could mean loss of income through loss of business opportunities for operations, growth and expansion. This is the limitation of the Cash Ratio. However, in case of organizations that have slow receivables collection or slow moving inventory, the Cash Ratio assumes importance.

A second drawback of the Cash Ratio is that since Marketable Securities would need to be converted into cash, the amount received would depend on market forces as the prices of Marketable Securities is volatile (changes day to day). Hence, the Cash Ratio needs to be calculated regularly as the ratio may change considerably with the changes in prices of Marketable Securities and hence once calculated, the ratio may not be valid over a period of time.

Cash Flow Ratio:

The Cash Flow Ratio measures the Cash Flow to the Current Liabilities. It calculates how many times more cash flow is generated as compared to the Current Liabilities. It is calculated as follows:

$$\frac{\text{Annual Cash Flow from Operations}}{\text{(Average) Current Liabilities}}$$

Some formulae use year end balances instead of Average Balances. When financial statements of multiple periods are available, average balances may be uses. In case information of a single period is available, year end balance may be used. This usually depends upon preference of the analyst.

The ideal Cash Flow Ratio is an annualized Cash Flow Ratio of 0.4 times. The term annualized implies that if the figure available for cash flow is for less than a year, it can be multiplied by the necessary figure to bring the amount to the annual cash flow. Say, the cash flow is available for only three months(it is a quarter. Three months make a quarter. Hence there are four quarters in a year); it can be multiplied by 4 to calculate the annual cash flow.

The Cash Flow Ratio analyzes the liquidity from the perspective of Cash Flow. Hence, if the working capital is positive but the cash from operations is insufficient to settle its dues, then borrowing money would be the only option to settle liabilities. This could work in the short term but over a long term, this could indicate solvency issues as financing will not always be available and even if it is available, it will not always be available on favorable terms. It is in the best interest to generate enough cash from operations to avoid such a scenario.

A high Cash Flow Ratio indicates a strong ability to repay obligations in the ordinary course of business whereas a low Cash Flow ratio could mean liquidity issues and a need to borrow. A low Cash Flow Ratio over a period of time could indicate risk of default and a probability of insolvency.

Net Working Capital Ratio:

The Net Working Capital Ratio calculates the Net Working Capital to the Total Assets. It is calculated as follows:

$$\frac{\text{Net Working Capital}}{\text{Total Assets}}$$

Net Working Capital can also be renamed as Net Liquid Assets and Total Assets can also be renamed as Total Capitalization. This ratio calculates whether there is enough Working Capital as compared to Total Assets. Thus this ratio measures liquidity by evaluating the ability to meet current obligations by maintaining sufficient Working Capital. This ratio also helps to evaluate whether the firm has enough Working Capital to expand its business.

The Net Working Capital Ratio helps comparison across years. It helps comparison with the ratios of previous years. This comparison assumes more significance when the ratio is decreasing. A decrease in the Net Working Capital Ratio through time signifies decrease in Working Capital and could be indicative of liquidity problems as well as insolvency.

The Net Working Capital Ratio also turns negative in case of negative Working Capital. Negative working capital means Current Liabilities exceed Current Assets. In the short term, a negative Net Working Capital Ratio may be acceptable but over a long term, a negative ratio indicates serious business problems that could lead to insolvency.

The Net Working Capital Ratio is not only dependent on the liquidity of Current Assets but also the liquidity of Current Liabilities. The liquidity of Current Liabilities is to be evaluated as well. The urgency of payment of Current Liabilities is to be evaluated. Tax liabilities, Payroll as well as Payments to Suppliers will be urgent or top priorities over other payments. There are some liabilities that are unrecorded in the books of accounts. These would also have to be taken into account. Commitments arising from Operating Leases and Purchase commitments would be such unrecorded obligations. Payments of any loan taken would also assume importance. Any default in payment of loan installments could mean the whole debt due immediately or legal action that could involve restructuring or insolvency proceedings.

Sometimes, the need is to look beyond the numbers of the books of accounts and adjust opinion to reflect the actual condition of the company and this condition could be extremely different to the one portrayed in the books of accounts.

REFERENCES:
1)http://pages.stern.nyu.edu/~%20adamodar/New_Home_Page/AccPrimer/inventory.htm
2)Irvin N. Gleim, Dale L. Flesher(2012) – Financial Planning, Performance and Control (Part 1), Gleim CMA Review, Sixteenth Edition.
3)Irvin N. Gleim, Dale L. Flesher(2012) – Financial Decision Making (Part 2), Gleim CMA Review, Sixteenth Edition.
4)Brian Hock, Lynn Roden, David Fairchild (2010) – Part 2 Financial Decision Making, Hock International.
5)Saurav Dutta, Tony Griffin, Karen L. Jett, Jan Kooiman, Lon Petro, Siaw-Peng Wan (2009) – CMA Learning System Part 2: Financial Decision Making, Version 3.0, Institute of Management Accountants (IMA).
6)Risk Management Association (2011) – Annual Statement Studies Financial Ratio Benchmarks 2011 2012 (www.rmahq.org).
7)Standards for the Calculation of Financial Ratios (2004)- The Danish Society of Financial Analysts, The Norwegian Society of Financial Analysts.
8)http://www.accountingcycle.org/Operating-Cycle.html
9)P Muralidhar (nd) – Ratio Analysis, Matrusri Institute of PG Studies, http://www.slideshare.net/Dharan178/ratio-analysis-2970642
10)http://www.qfinance.com/cash-flow-management-calculations/liquidity-ratio-analysis

11)http://www.allprojectreports.com/MBA-Projects/Finance-Project-Report/ratio-analysis/ratio-analysis-advantage-limitations-classification-financial-ratio-analysis.htm

12)http://www.demonstratingvalue.org/resources/financial-ratio-analysis

13)http://www3.nd.edu/~mgrecon/simulations/micromaticweb/financialratios.html

14)http://www.cliffsnotes.com/more-subjects/accounting/accounting-principles-ii/financial-statement-analysis/ratio-analysis

15)http://www.bized.co.uk/compfact/ratios/liquid1.htm

16)http://www.demonstratingvalue.org/resources/financial-ratio-analysis#Leverage

17)http://www.demonstratingvalue.org/resources/financial-ratio-analysis#Profitability

18)http://www.bized.co.uk/compfact/ratios/investor10.htm

19)http://en.wikibooks.org/wiki/AQA_Business_Studies/Ratio_Analysis

20)http://www.prenhall.com/divisions/bp/app/cfl/RA/MarketValueRatios.html

21)http://www.prenhall.com/divisions/bp/app/cfl/RA/DebtManagementRatios.html

22)http://www.investopedia.com/terms/s/shareholdersequity.asp

23)http://www.bized.co.uk/compfact/ratios/asset5.htm

24)Hemant R. Dani (2000) – Balance Sheets Content, Analysis and Interpretation, Vision Books Pvt Ltd.

PROFITABILITY RATIOS

The profitability of an organization is important for the long term survival of an organization as well as to determine the level of profits earned. Profitability Ratios determine the ability to generate revenues after taking into consideration the expenses as well as other relevant costs that have been incurred during a certain amount of time under consideration.

Almost all Profitability Ratios that have a high value (either as compared with previous figures or as compared to figures of competitors in the same industry or sector) are more desirable. This would indicate that the company is doing better than before or better than its competitors. Profitability Ratios are the most widely used ratios in the business world for the purpose of understanding the profitability of an organization and for generation of shareholder value and are very widely understood and used by the public at large.

Some Profitability Ratios are affected by season. An example would be the retail industry. The retail industry could generate high revenue during festive times like Christmas, Diwali, Thanksgiving in America etc.

There are various Profitability Ratios. Some of them are Gross Profit Ratio, Net Profit Ratio, Operating Profit Margin Ratio, EBITDA (Earnings Before Interest, Taxes, Depreciation and Amortization) Margin Ratio.

Gross Profit Margin Ratio:

Gross Profit Margin Ratio measures the percentage of Gross Profit in relation to total Sales and is expressed in terms of percentage (%). It takes into consideration whether all expenses are covered by the Revenues earned. Gross Profit is calculated as Sales less Cost of Goods Sold. It is calculated as follows:

$$\frac{Gross\ Profit}{Net\ Sales}$$

It can also be rewritten as

$$\frac{Net\ Sales - Cost\ of\ Goods\ Sold}{Net\ Sales}$$

Net Sales is calculates as Sales less any Sales Discounts. Sales Returns as well as any Sales Allowances are also to be deducted from Sales. In case there are no Sales Returns or discounts given during Sales, then Sales figure is to be assumed to be Net Sales.

Gross Profit Ratio is a very important ratio. It measures whether all costs have been covered as well as whether there is any leftover income after accounting for all costs. The Gross Profit Ratio is therefore a key ratio for any organization.

A change in the Gross Profit Ratio is usually due to change in selling price per unit, change in number of units sold as well as increase or decrease in the costs per unit. In order to determine the reason for change in the Gross Profit Ratio, Variance Analysis is usually performed. The causes behind the variance also need to be assessed and addressed in order to increase profitability.

Possible reasons for the change in the Gross Profit Ratio could include change in sales prices as compared to change in inventory costs. Another reason could be change in volume of sales due to economic factors such as recession, growth, competition etc. The product mix that is sold could have altered. Generally companies with more than one product may not sell the same quantity of each product in every period. As the quantity of each product sold will differ in each period, the Gross Profit Ratio will also change. Loss of inventory due to natural factors, theft, normal and abnormal spoilage, decay, obsolescence and even low inventory levels could result in lost sales and hence, low profits.

Organizations in the service industry may not have a Cost of Goods Sold. In such cases, expenses such as Cost of Merchandise could be used as Cost of Goods Sold. However, in service organizations, the Gross Profit Ratio is not of high importance.

However the limitation is that all the information needed to calculate the Gross Profit Ratio is not easily available to outsiders. Information such as number of units sold, the cost of the units, the selling price of each unit sold etc is not available to any individual or entity outside the organization. This ratio is best calculated outside the company. An outsider must depend on the figure declared by the company in the books of accounts. Moreover, an organization may not be able to fully control its costs due to market forces at play that may drive costs up and thereby reduce profits.

Operating Profit Margin Ratio:

Operating Profit Margin Ratio measures how much revenue out of total sales is being retained by way of Operating Income. It is expressed in terms of Percentage (%). It is calculated as follows:

Operating Income

Net Sales

Operating Income can be defined as the expenses and revenues that arise from the operations of the organization. Income Taxes are also a part of Operating Expenses. However, only the principal operations are taken into account any auxiliary activity's expenses or revenues. Similarly, revenues or expenses from discontinued operations are also not taken into account.

The Operating Profit Margin Ratio is often seen together with the Gross Profit Ratio as the Operating Profit Margin Ratio includes the operating expenses of the organization. If the Gross Profit Ratio is high and the Operating Profit Margin Ratio is low or negative, it could indicate that operating expenses are high and need to be controlled. In case the Gross Profit Ratio and the Operating Profit Margin Ratio are both positive and show a healthy trend, it could mean the operating expenses are controlled and there is efficiency in operations.

Reasons for the change in Operating Profit Margin Ratio should be analyzed. In case the Operating Profit Margin Ratio is showing an increasing trend, it could indicate a particular efficiency that could be developed further. In case the Operating Profit Margin shows a declining trend, it indicates rising costs and possible inefficiencies in operations that need to be analyzed and corrected. Over a period of time, a declining Operating Profit Margin Ratio can be cause for concern that could result in default and even bankruptcy.

There is a healthy argument in the financial world as to whether the Operating Profit Margin is meaningful or not especially for companies that have unusual items in the books of accounts. The argument for using the Operating Profit Margin is that the Operating Profit Margin represents income from continuing operations and is therefore indicative of what may happen in the future. The argument against using the Operating Profit Margin is that unusual items are almost always present in the books of accounts and therefore, net income is a better indicator.

Another problem with the Operating Profit Margin is with respect to the classification of the items into unusual items and items from ongoing operations. There are companies that try to classify items in such a way that income from operations is kept as high as possible.

EBITDA (Earnings Before Interest, Taxes, Depreciation and Amortization) Margin Ratio:

EBITDA (Earnings Before Interest, Taxes, Depreciation and Amortization) Margin Ratio takes into consideration the Operating Income Before Taxes (EBIT) and adds to it Amortization as well as Depreciation. This ratio is used as a measure of operating profitability and non operating expenses such as interest, depreciation, amortization, taxes are not taken into consideration in this ratio. This ratio is expressed in term of percentage (%). It is calculated as follows:

EBITDA (Earnings Before Interest, Taxes, Depreciation and Amortization)

Net Sales

EBITDA (Earnings Before Interest, Taxes, Depreciation and Amortization) Margin Ratio could be the only indicator with respect to the future earning power in the short term. This ratio can only be used during the short term. For long term profitability, other ratios need to be taken into consideration and basing any decision on this ratio alone would be fallacious. This is due to the fact that any organization needs to show real earnings at some time and for that purpose, EBITDA (Earnings Before Interest, Taxes, Depreciation and Amortization) Margin Ratio is not an appropriate measure. This ratio is also used to compare between companies as well as compare companies against an industry average.

There is a lot of criticism attached to the EBITDA (Earnings Before Interest, Taxes, Depreciation and Amortization) Margin Ratio. The addition of Depreciation and Amortization does not make it a Cash Flow. When Interest, Taxes, Depreciation and Amortization are not taken into consideration, unprofitable organizations may seem to be profitable. Thus, this ratio may be able to manipulate profitability.

For any organization to remain profitable, it must not only cover its cash charges but its non cash charges as well. It is not enough to cover only the cost of goods sold and the charges for the administrative functioning of the company. Profits have to be made available towards capital spending as well if the intention is growth and expansion.

The exclusion of a non cash charge such as depreciation can be used to understate the requirements of profits as well as the costs of the functioning of the organization.

Fixed Assets are depreciated. If this depreciation is ignored or not taken into consideration, the need to set cash aside to buy fixed assets in the future is also ignored and this can cause great problems when the fixed asset is fully depreciated and there is an urgent need to buy new fixed assets. The result will be that the firm will not be as competitive as it could have been had it taken non cash expenses into account while making decisions.

Capital Spending must also therefore be taken into consideration if the company has to truly take into account all its costs.

In order for a ratio such as EBITDA (Earnings Before Interest, Taxes, Depreciation and Amortization) Margin Ratio to be truly meaningful, the organization that is being evaluated must be genuinely profitable. This ratio is better suited for the evaluation of old line industrial firms. In such cases, the results produced would be more meaningful.

Earnings Before Interest and Taxes (EBIT) Ratio:

The Earnings Before Interest and Taxes (EBIT) Ratio compares the Earnings Before Interest and Taxes (EBIT) to Sales (Revenue). It is calculated as follows:

<u>Earnings Before Interest and Taxes (EBIT)</u>

Net Sales (Revenue)

The Earnings Before Interest and Taxes (EBIT) Ratio is used along with the EBITDA (Earnings Before Interest, Taxes, Depreciation and Amortization) Margin Ratio.

However, in case impairment tests are done on goodwill, the Earnings Before Interest and Taxes (EBIT) Ratio becomes less useful than the EBITDA (Earnings Before Interest, Taxes,

Depreciation and Amortization) Margin Ratio as the EBITDA (Earnings Before Interest, Taxes, Depreciation and Amortization) Margin Ratio will equal the Earnings Before Interest and Taxes (EBIT) Ratio.

Earnings Before Tax (EBT) Ratio:

The Earnings Before Tax (EBT) Ratio compares the Earnings Before Tax (EBT) and Sales. It is calculated as follows:

Earnings Before Taxes (EBT)

Net Sales (Revenue)

The Earnings Before Tax (EBT) Ratio is also known as the Pre Tax Margin. The Earnings Before Tax (EBT) Ratio gives an idea about the increase or decrease in profitability of an organization through the years.

However, the limitation of the Earnings Before Tax (EBT) Ratio is that there tends to be a distortion of the Earnings Before Tax (EBT) Ratio in case of significant change in the capital structure of the organization. Due to this limitation, the Earnings Before Tax (EBT) Ratio is not extremely useful when comparing different organizations. The Earnings Before Tax (EBT) Ratio is also not useful for online consolidated associated organizations.

Net Profit Margin Ratio:

Net Profit Margin includes the total profitability of the company taking into consideration expenses as well as revenues from all sources. Comprehensive Income items are not included in this ratio as they are included in the Statement of Equity. It is expressed in terms of percentage (%). It is calculated as follows:

Net Income

Net Sales

This is also a highly popular ratio among the insiders in the company as well individuals and entities outside the organization. This ratio takes into consideration whether the company as a whole is profitable taking into consideration all the incomes and expenses as a whole, not just manufacturing or operating revenues and expenses. It takes into consideration whether each and every item of expense is covered by revenues and if there is something left over for distribution to investors and shareholder and/or for reinvestment in the company for growth and expansion.

The Net Profit Margin is to be taken into consideration along with the Gross Profit Ratio and the Operating Profit Margin Ratio and reasons for an increasing as well as declining trend need to be analyzed.

Cash Earnings Ratio:

The Cash Earnings Ratio is calculated as follows:

(Net Profit + Amortization + Depreciation + Expensed Share Based Payments + Write Downs)

Share in Associates

Share of Minorities in Amortization, Depreciation, Expensed Share Based Payments

The Cash Earnings Ratio is calculated by dividing Net Profit, Amortization, Depreciation, Expensed Share Based Payments, Write Downs by Share in Associates which is in turn divided by Share of Minorities in Amortization, Depreciation, Expensed Share Based Payments

The Cash Earnings Ratio is to be differentiated from Cash Flow as the Cash Earnings Ratio does not take into account net working capital as well as capital expenditures.

The adjustments made are that of excluding the effect of the share of minorities in depreciation, amortization as well as expensed share based payments. This is done to calculate the Cash Earnings Ratio for the post minorities' level. Non cash items such as changes in provisions (for calculation of cash earnings) may be included in some situations.

Sales Growth Ratio:

The Sales Growth Ratio compares the sales or revenue of the current period with the sales or revenue of the previous or past periods. It is calculated as follows:

Current Period Sales or Revenue– Previous Period Sales or Revenue

Previous Period Sales or Revenue

The Sales Growth Ratio gives an idea about the percentage of increase or decrease in sales or revenue over a period of time. The current period's sales or revenue can be compared to the past periods and the rate of increase or decrease in sales or revenue can be obtained.

In case the overall costs are increasing, the sales or revenue has to also increase in proportion or greater than the increase in costs. In case inflation is rising, the sales or revenue has to also increase in proportion or greater than the increase in the rate of inflation. If this is not the case, the pricing policy of the products or services needs to be checked and revised.

Reliance on Revenue Source Ratio:

The Reliance on Revenue Ratio compares the Revenue from a particular source with the Total Revenue. It is calculated as follows:

$$\frac{\text{Total Revenue from a Particular Source}}{\text{Total Revenue of the Organization}}$$

The Reliance on Revenue Ratio gives an idea about the revenue generated from a particular source as compared to the total revenue. This gives an idea about the reliance of the organization on particular sources of revenue.

The Reliance on Revenue Ratio can be used to analyze the nature as well as the risk that is associated with each revenue source thus helping the organization understand various factors such as the seasonality or permanence of the revenue source, market share (whether it is growing or not), the contracts associated with each revenue source etc.

The Reliance on Revenue Ratio is usually used to determine short term trends as well as long term trends and align them with the strategic funding goals so as to rely less on outside sources of finance and a move towards self sufficiency.

REFERENCES:

1)http://pages.stern.nyu.edu/~%20adamodar/New_Home_Page/AccPrimer/inventory.htm
2)Irvin N. Gleim, Dale L. Flesher(2012) – Financial Planning, Performance and Control (Part 1), Gleim CMA Review, Sixteenth Edition.
3)Irvin N. Gleim, Dale L. Flesher(2012) – Financial Decision Making (Part 2), Gleim CMA Review, Sixteenth Edition.
4)Brian Hock, Lynn Roden, David Fairchild (2010) – Part 2 Financial Decision Making, Hock International.
5)Saurav Dutta, Tony Griffin, Karen L. Jett, Jan Kooiman, Lon Petro, Siaw-Peng Wan (2009) – CMA Learning System Part 2: Financial Decision Making, Version 3.0, Institute of Management Accountants (IMA).
6)Risk Management Association (2011) – Annual Statement Studies Financial Ratio Benchmarks 2011 2012 (www.rmahq.org).
7)Standards for the Calculation of Financial Ratios (2004)- The Danish Society of Financial Analysts, The Norwegian Society of Financial Analysts.
8)http://www.accountingcycle.org/Operating-Cycle.html
9)P Muralidhar (nd) – Ratio Analysis, Matrusri Institute of PG Studies, http://www.slideshare.net/Dharan178/ratio-analysis-2970642
10)http://www.qfinance.com/cash-flow-management-calculations/liquidity-ratio-analysis
11)http://www.allprojectreports.com/MBA-Projects/Finance-Project-Report/ratio-analysis/ratio-analysis-advantage-limitations-classification-financial-ratio-analysis.htm
12)http://www.demonstratingvalue.org/resources/financial-ratio-analysis
13)http://www3.nd.edu/~mgrecon/simulations/micromaticweb/financialratios.html
14)http://www.cliffsnotes.com/more-subjects/accounting/accounting-principles-ii/financial-statement-analysis/ratio-analysis
15)http://www.bized.co.uk/compfact/ratios/liquid1.htm
16)http://www.demonstratingvalue.org/resources/financial-ratio-analysis#Leverage
17)http://www.demonstratingvalue.org/resources/financial-ratio-analysis#Profitability
18)http://www.bized.co.uk/compfact/ratios/investor10.htm

19)http://en.wikibooks.org/wiki/AQA_Business_Studies/Ratio_Analysis
20)http://www.prenhall.com/divisions/bp/app/cfl/RA/MarketValueRatios.html
21)http://www.prenhall.com/divisions/bp/app/cfl/RA/DebtManagementRatios.html
22)http://www.investopedia.com/terms/s/shareholdersequity.asp
23)http://www.bized.co.uk/compfact/ratios/asset5.htm
24)Hemant R. Dani (2000) – Balance Sheets Content, Analysis and Interpretation, Vision Books Pvt Ltd.

LEVERAGE RATIOS

Leverage can be defined as the ability to generate higher return when compared to the capital or cost incurred for the project. Therefore, if returns are high when compared to the cost, it is advantageous to have some leverage.

Capital Structure of an organization includes Equity Capital as well as Debt. Therefore, Capital Structure can be seen as the way the organization chooses to do business through financing of operations and expansion activities. Any organization has a choice. It can issue equity or it may incur debt to finance its activities. The choice an organization makes will depend on many factors.

If the organization issues equity, as and when the profits are sufficient, dividends may be declared. There is no compulsion however to pay dividend. Moreover, money received by issuance of equity need not be repaid. But since the number of shares issued increases, the voting rights are diluted. Debt on the other hand is a cost. Interest on debt needs to be repaid at regular intervals as agreed. Moreover, the principal amount of the debt also needs to be repaid as specified by the maturity date. But the voting rights are not diluted.

The decision (debt or equity) that the organization makes will affect the ability of the organization to make future decisions. However, no decision is right or wrong. The aim of any organization is to obtain finance in the cheapest possible way while maximizing profits. The more financing that an organization already has, the more costly any additional financing will be to the organization.

The debt or equity proportion in the Capital Structure assumes importance in Solvency Analysis. Solvency refers to the ability of an organization to repay debt and other long term obligations as and when they become due. This is to be distinguished from liquidity as liquidity refers to the ability of the organization to repay short term obligations whereas solvency refers to the ability to repay long term obligations.

In addition to the influence Of Capital Structure, solvency of any organization is also influenced by the profits made through operations as it is through profits that payments can be made towards principal amount of the debt as well as interest payments on debt. Therefore, solvency is dependent on the quality of profits or earnings and the ability of the earnings to cover repayment of debt.

Since debt needs to be repaid, more profits are required to cover the debt payments. An organization that has more equity in the capital need not repay the money received and hence is able to take on more risk. Debt is more unstable to have in the Capital Structure as in case of default on payment of interest or principal amount, the debt can be recalled. Moreover covenants can be imposed on the organization for the continuation of debt financing such as maintenance of a particular Current Ratio, Long Term Debt Ratio etc. Failure to comply with such covenants may cause the entire debt to be repaid at once. Hence an organization with more equity as compared to debt is considered to be more financially stable and hence more able to be solvent.

If an organization has more debt as compared to equity as part of its Capital Structure, more assets would be required to be generated in order to payments towards interest payments as well as payment towards the principal amount. Hence, the solvency of such an organization is considered to be lower as payments towards interest payments as well as payment towards the principal amount may have a negative or a positive impact on the future earnings of the organization. In case the impact is negative, the solvency and liquidity of the organization may be a risk and the risk of default and insolvency may be high.

The Capital Structure of an organization is not rigid. It can be changed. Long term debt may be paid off, more equity could be issued thus improving solvency. Convertible bonds can be converted into equity. This will again increase the solvency of the organization and decreasing the risk of insolvency and default. The organization can also attempt to increase debt rather than equity by borrowing money and repurchasing treasury stock. This has the effect of increasing debt and hence decreasing the solvency the organization and increasing the risk of insolvency and default.

Leverage Ratio can be calculated as follows:

Pre Fixed Cost Income Amount

Post Fixed Cost Income Amount

Leverage is of two types: Operating Leverage and Financial Leverage.

Degree of Operating Leverage Ratio:

Degree of Operating Leverage Ratio measures the effect on profits due to the operating leverage. It is calculated as follows:

% Change in Operating Income (EBIT)

% Change in Sales

It can also be calculated as follows:

Contribution Margin

Operating Income (EBIT)

The formula using the percentage change in Operating Income to the percentage change in Sales can be calculated when financial reports are made with Absorption Costing. The Operating Leverage calculates the percentage change in profits in relation to a percentage change in sales. Operating Leverage takes into account the fixed operating costs that need to be taken into account and need to be paid before making a profit. The change in profits being of a higher percentage than a percentage change in sales is known as Operating Leverage.

Thus, the Operating Leverage is used to measure the operating fixed cost in order to generate higher profit. Fixed Costs are costs that remain constant over a relevant range of activity. In the long run, out of the relevant range of activity, all costs are variable.

However, within the relevant range, some costs do not change with the production level and they are to be incurred even if there is no production activity at all. Examples of such costs are rent of premises, salaries of managers. These are fixed costs within a relevant range of activity.

And since these costs do not change with change in level of production, change in volume of sales will cause a change in level of profits after deduction of fixed costs. It can thus be seen that if fixed expenses are high, the operating expenses will be high and thus the operating leverage will be high.

Profits are calculated after deduction of fixed costs from the contribution margin.

Contribution Margin is calculated as follows:

Sales
-Variable Costs

So, if the Variable Costs are higher than Sales, there will be a loss. Even if revenue from sales is enough to cover Variable Costs, if Fixed Costs are higher than the Contribution Margin, there will be a loss. But, once Contribution Margin is sufficient to cover Fixed Costs (known as Break Even Point), any increase in revenue from Sales will increase the Contribution Margin and therefore will lead to an increase in Profits. For an organization with high Operating Leverage, the effect on Operating Income will high with change in level of Sales. If Sales increase, the increase in Operating Income will be magnified whereas if Sales decrease, the decrease in Operating Income will also be magnified.

An example of an organization having high Operating Leverage would be that of an organization involved in the production of highly automated machines. In such an organization, Fixed Costs would be high as the costs of the equipment would be high. The Variable Costs for labor would also be on the lower side as labor as a cost of production would be less required.

When a company is near Break Even Point, chances of Profits in relation to change in Sales are high as compared to a company that is operating above or below the Break Even Point. This is due to the fact that when an organization is operating above or below the Break Even Point, even though the magnification effect of Operating Leverage is present, the magnification effect is not pronounced.

When two or more organizations are compared for their operating results, the organization that has higher Fixed Expenses will have higher Operating Leverage assuming that all other things are equal.

The Degree of Operating Leverage Ratio should not be considered as a static measurement. The ratio changes with changing level of sales. The Degree of Operating Leverage Ratio gets larger with each increase in the level of sales until the sales approach the Break Even Point. This is because at the Break Even Point, the costs equal total revenue from sales and hence, the operating income is zero.

The Degree of Operating Leverage Ratio can only be calculated for companies whose financial are based on the Variable Costing method as the Operating Margin and Contribution Margin need to be calculated. This ratio can be easily calculated by someone with access to internal records which specify the fixed costs and the variable costs.

Absorption Costing does not allow for separation of the fixed costs from the variable costs. Calculation of the Operating Leverage Ratio based on financial statements that are prepared with absorption costing as the basis will be possible when income statements of two years are available. In such a case, the Operating Leverage Ratio can be calculated through the use of % change in sales and % change in operating income.

High degree of Operating Leverage indicates a high risk as the fixed costs tend to be high and these fixed costs need to be covered regardless of the level of sales. Similarly, low degree of Operating Leverage indicates a low risk as the fixed costs tend to be low. However, a high Operating Leverage may also indicate greater ability to expand rapidly when the demand for the organization's product(s) is high.

Operating Leverage tends to explain the sensitivity of the Operating Income in relation to Sales Volume. The higher the Operating Leverage, the greater is the sensitivity of the Operating Income in relation to Sales Volume. Similarly, the lower the Operating Leverage, the lesser is the sensitivity of the Operating Income in relation to Sales Volume.

Degree of Financial Leverage Ratio:

The Degree of Financial Leverage Ratio measures the effect of any change in Earnings Before Interest and Tax (EBIT) on Net Income. It is calculated as follows:

% Change in Net income

% Change in Earnings Before Interest and Taxes (EBIT)

It can also be calculated as follows:

Earnings Before Interest and Taxes (EBIT)

Earnings Before Taxes(EBT)

The formula that uses percentage change in Net Income compared to percentage change in Earnings Before Interest and Taxes (EBIT) can be used when financial information over two or more periods is available. The formula using Earnings Before Interest and Taxes (EBIT) compared to Earnings Before Taxes(EBT) can be used when information of a single period is available.

Financial Leverage signifies the use of debt in order to increase revenue. The debt is used for creation of new business opportunities or for operational purposes. When debt is used, interest is paid on the debt as consideration for the debt. Unlike dividends, which can be issued as and when profits are available, interest is a fixed expense. It needs to be paid whether the company is making profits or not.

Therefore, the use of debt carries a fixed charge and this is known as Financial Leverage. Financial Leverage can therefore also be defined as the percentage of debt (fixed cost) that is used as a means of finance due to the increase in financial costs (repayment of interest as well as principal of the debt) to the company.

Financial Leverage is a part of Financing when it comes to calculation of the Statement of Cash Flows. Financial Leverage Ratios are used to measure the debt used by an organization in order to finance operations and/or the assets. Hence, it is used as a part of solvency analysis. Financial Leverage has the effect of magnifying the success (profits) or failure (loss) due to the managerial decision of using debt.

The Financial Leverage as part of the capital structure will magnify the effect of any change in Earnings Before Interest and Taxes (EBIT) on the Net Income (NI). The higher the Earnings Before Interest and Taxes (EBIT) the higher the Net Income (NI). Similarly, the lower the Earnings Before Interest and Taxes (EBIT) the lower the Net Income (NI).

Higher Financial Leverage indicates higher risk as the fixed costs are higher and there is a risk that the company may not be able to pay its debt and even of insolvency in case the company keeps defaulting on debt regularly. On the other hand, higher Financial Leverage also indicates an opportunity to the organization for increase in revenue and profits which means that the company will be able to pay off the fixed debt and generate higher profits leaving the shareholders better off than before. In such a case, there will be benefits from the Financial Leverage. Use of Financial Leverage therefore requires careful consideration from management.

A Financial Leverage Ratio of 2.0 implies that the equity of the organization is equal to its debt. A Financial Leverage Ratio greater than 2.0 implies that debt (liabilities) is greater than equity. A Financial Leverage Ratio lesser than 2.0 implies that debt (liabilities) is lesser than equity

One advantage of using Financial Leverage is that the interest expense is tax deductible. Since tax payment is reduced, the burden of interest is proportionately reduced. Another advantage of using Financial Leverage is that the return earned from the investment of the debt capital (Return on Assets) exceeds the interest paid on debt thus increasing profits substantially and benefitting the equity share holders.

The formula with the figures of percentage Change in Net Income and percentage Change in Earnings Before Interest and Taxes (EBIT) can only be calculated if financial information of two or more years is available. The second formula with the figure of Earnings Before Interest and Taxes (EBIT) and Earnings Before Taxes (EBT) can be used when figures of a single period or multiple periods are available.

The Degree of Financial Leverage Ratio is based on the fact that interest paid on debt is a fixed expense. Degree of The Financial Leverage Ratio is calculated at a particular level of interest expense and income. When the level of income and interest on debt change, the Financial Leverage Ratio will change as well.

The Degree of Financial Leverage Ratio is therefore a measurement of change in Earnings Before Interest and Taxes (EBIT) in relation to a change in Earnings Before Taxes (EBT). The assumption is that Interest Expense remains constant. When debt is taken, financial leverage rises and payment of interest on debt becomes necessary. Therefore, when debt rises, the financial leverage rises and when debt decreases, financial leverage decreases. Once the fixed Interest Expense is deducted from Earnings Before Interest and Taxes (EBIT), any amount so remaining would therefore be the Earnings Before Taxes (EBT). Since the amount of Interest Expense does not change for a particular period, the change in Earnings Before Interest and Taxes (EBIT) has a direct effect on the Earnings Before Taxes (EBT).

As a consequence of this, when debt or financial leverage is used and assuming interest payment remains constant for a particular period, an increase in Earnings Before Interest and Taxes (EBIT) will result in an even greater increase in Earnings Before Taxes (EBT). Similarly, a decrease in Earnings Before Interest and Taxes (EBIT) will result in an even greater decrease in Earnings Before Taxes (EBT).

From the perspective of a shareholder, the Financial Leverage Ratio is an opportunity to gain funds for operations and expansion of the business resulting in higher profits and dividends as well as capital appreciation. However, there is an inherent risk in debt as well in the nature of interest payments and reduction in the Income Available to Common or Equity Shareholders or even non payment of debt and insolvency.

The higher the degree of Financial Leverage, the higher the multiplication factor for opportunity (positive) or risk (negative). Similarly, the lower the degree of Financial Leverage, the lower the multiplication factor for opportunity (positive) or for risk (negative). Thus it can be said that Financial Leverage has the effect of magnifying the effect on earnings in relation to the leverage.

REFERENCES:

1)http://pages.stern.nyu.edu/~%20adamodar/New_Home_Page/AccPrimer/inventory.htm
2)Irvin N. Gleim, Dale L. Flesher(2012) – Financial Planning, Performance and Control (Part 1), Gleim CMA Review, Sixteenth Edition.
3)Irvin N. Gleim, Dale L. Flesher(2012) – Financial Decision Making (Part 2), Gleim CMA Review, Sixteenth Edition.
4)Brian Hock, Lynn Roden, David Fairchild (2010) – Part 2 Financial Decision Making, Hock International.
5)Saurav Dutta, Tony Griffin, Karen L. Jett, Jan Kooiman, Lon Petro, Siaw-Peng Wan (2009) – CMA Learning System Part 2: Financial Decision Making, Version 3.0, Institute of Management Accountants (IMA).
6)Risk Management Association (2011) – Annual Statement Studies Financial Ratio Benchmarks 2011 2012 (www.rmahq.org).
7)Standards for the Calculation of Financial Ratios (2004)- The Danish Society of Financial Analysts, The Norwegian Society of Financial Analysts.
8)http://www.accountingcycle.org/Operating-Cycle.html
9)P Muralidhar (nd) – Ratio Analysis, Matrusri Institute of PG Studies, http://www.slideshare.net/Dharan178/ratio-analysis-2970642
10)http://www.qfinance.com/cash-flow-management-calculations/liquidity-ratio-analysis
11)http://www.allprojectreports.com/MBA-Projects/Finance-Project-Report/ratio-analysis/ratio-analysis-advantage-limitations-classification-financial-ratio-analysis.htm
12)http://www.demonstratingvalue.org/resources/financial-ratio-analysis
13)http://www3.nd.edu/~mgrecon/simulations/micromaticweb/financialratios.html
14)http://www.cliffsnotes.com/more-subjects/accounting/accounting-principles-ii/financial-statement-analysis/ratio-analysis
15)http://www.bized.co.uk/compfact/ratios/liquid1.htm
16)http://www.demonstratingvalue.org/resources/financial-ratio-analysis#Leverage
17)http://www.demonstratingvalue.org/resources/financial-ratio-analysis#Profitability
18)http://www.bized.co.uk/compfact/ratios/investor10.htm
19)http://en.wikibooks.org/wiki/AQA_Business_Studies/Ratio_Analysis
20)http://www.prenhall.com/divisions/bp/app/cfl/RA/MarketValueRatios.html
21)http://www.prenhall.com/divisions/bp/app/cfl/RA/DebtManagementRatios.html
22)http://www.investopedia.com/terms/s/shareholdersequity.asp
23)http://www.bized.co.uk/compfact/ratios/asset5.htm
24)Hemant R. Dani (2000) – Balance Sheets Content, Analysis and Interpretation, Vision Books Pvt Ltd.

COVERAGE RATIOS

Coverage Ratios give an idea about the ability of an organization to meet its debt obligations. Coverage Ratios give an indication about the ability of an organization to meet debt from the profit (income) arising from operations. Coverage Ratios differ from Liquidity Ratios. Liquidity Ratios emphasize on the possibility of liquidation of an organization and the ability of an organization to avoid liquidation and stay in business. Coverage Ratios emphasize on the ability of an organization to continue as a viable business enterprise and the ability to pay its debt and creditors.

Coverage Ratios can be classified into two types namely the Asset Coverage Ratios and the Earnings Coverage Ratios.

Asset Coverage Ratios:

Asset Coverage Ratios are very important from the point of view of the creditors. Creditors are more interested in the assets as they want to ensure that they get their money back. Hence, they look to the assets to determine the earning power as well as to determine the value of the assets in case of liquidation in order to determine how much they can get back in this scenario. Fixed Assets to Equity Capital, Net Tangible Assets to Long Term Debt and Total Liabilities to Net Tangible Assets are the Asset Coverage Ratios.

Fixed Assets to Equity Capital Ratio:

Fixed Assets to Equity Capital Ratio gives an idea about the Fixed Assets in relation to the Equity Capital of the organization. It is calculated as follows:

Net Fixed Assets

Total Equity

Fixed Assets to Equity Capital Ratio gives a fair idea as to the amount of Equity Capital that is invested in the Fixed Assets. Investment in Fixed Assets means lesser funds available for operating purposes. However, it also means that it is these Fixed Assets that will generate revenue. A Fixed Assets to Equity Capital Ratio of less than 1.00 is considered favorable as this means that Equity Capital has been used to finance Fixed Assets and there is something remaining by way of operating funds as well. A Fixed Assets to Equity Capital Ratio greater than 1.00 means that Fixed Assets exceed Equity Capital. This means that apart from Equity, debt has also been used to finance Fixed Assets. Debt implies that interest payments along with principal will have to be repaid, reducing funds available for operation.

Net Tangible Assets to Long Term Debt Ratio:

The Net Tangible Assets to Long Term Debt Ratio gives an indication as to the coverage of Assets as compared to the Long Term Debt. Long Term Debt implies debt of a long term nature. It is calculated as follows:

$$\frac{\text{Total Assets} - \text{Tangible Assets} - \text{Total Liabilities}}{\text{Long Term Debt}}$$

In the Net Tangible Assets to Long Term Debt Ratio, only the tangible assets are taken into consideration. Thus by very definition, intangible assets such as Goodwill are excluded from the calculation of this ratio. One reason for the exclusion of intangible assets is that their value in the event of liquidation is very difficult to predict. Net Tangible Assets includes the Working Capital.

The Net Tangible Assets to Long Term Debt Ratio makes an assumption that in the event of liquidation, the liquidation value will be equal to the net book value of the asset. This may not always be the case. Some assets may have a value at liquidation that is much lesser than its net book value. Other assets may have values at liquidation that are at great variation with respect to the net book value (net of depreciation) as stated in the books of account. Hence, this assumption may not always be correct.

Total Liabilities to Tangible Assets Ratio:

The Total Liabilities to Tangible Assets Ratio measures the ratio of Total Liabilities to Tangible Assets. It is calculated as follows:

$$\frac{\text{Total Liabilities}}{\text{Total Assets} - \text{Tangible Assets} - \text{Total Liabilities}}$$

The Total Liabilities to Tangible Assets Ratio takes into consideration all the liabilities (current as well as long term) and compares them with total assets. The Total Liabilities to Tangible Assets Ratio will therefore indicate whether all liabilities will be able to be met with the tangible assets or will the organization have to borrow more.

Earnings Coverage Ratios:

Earnings Coverage Ratios assess the earning power as it is through earnings that payments for interest as well as the principal of the debt is paid. It is through earnings that growth and expansion is achieved. If earnings are not enough, there may be difficulty in repayment of debt and chances of default increase. Earnings Coverage Ratios help assess whether earnings are enough to cover fixed charges such as interest as well as other debt obligations. Therefore, calculation of Earnings Coverage Ratios assumes significance. There are three Earnings Ratios that are calculated, they are Interest Coverage Ratio, Fixed Charge Coverage Ratio, Cash Flow to Fixed Charges Ratio.

Interest Coverage Ratio:

The Interest Coverage Ratio is also known as the Times Interest Earned Ratio. The Interest Coverage Ratio measures whether Earnings are sufficient to pay the interest expense on the debt outstanding. It is calculated as follows:

$$\frac{\text{Earnings Before Interest and Taxes (EBIT)}}{\text{Interest Expense}}$$

The Interest Coverage Ratio gives a good indication of the ability of the company to pay interest on debt from the earnings of the company. Since interest is a tax deductible item of expenditure, the figure of Earnings Before Interest and Taxes (EBIT) is to be taken in the calculation of the Interest Coverage Ratio. Unusual items, items of an extraordinary nature, infrequent items, effects of accounting changes, discontinued operations should be adjusted in the calculation of Earnings Before Interest and Taxes (EBIT). The adjustment has to take place as these items are not recurring in nature and they are not a part of ordinary operations of the organization. They arise very infrequently and are not a good indicator of earnings from operations.

Since the Interest Coverage Ratio measures the ability of Earnings Before Interest and Taxes (EBIT) to cover interest expense, a ratio on the higher side is considered good. An Interest Coverage Ratio of 3.00 and above is extremely desirable whereas an Interest Coverage Ratio of 1.5 signifies a significant risk in meeting interest expense. An Interest Coverage Ratio below 1.5 signifies that the risk of default has increased substantially.

The Times Interest Earned Ratio should be at least 2 to 3 times. In case the Times Interest Earned Ratio is less than 2 times, the ability to get a loan from banks and financial institutions is affected adversely.

Although the inability to pay principal amount of debt is a cause for serious concern, any organization facing operational problems that result in cash flow issues can still stay operational as long as interest payments are made on time. The Interest Coverage Ratio therefore assumes importance.

If the Interest Coverage Ratio is low and the Debt to Equity Ratio, Total Debt to Total Capital and Total Debt to Total Capital Ratio are high, it could indicate default and possibility of insolvency if the trend continues over a period of time.

On the other hand, if the Interest Coverage Ratio is high and the Debt to Equity Ratio, Total Debt to Total Capital and Total Debt to Total Capital Ratio are also high, there is not a high chance of default or insolvency. A high Interest Coverage Ratio can also mean that additional debt obligations can be taken for growth and expansion purposes.

A criticism of the Interest Coverage Ratio is that it does not take into consideration operating lease obligations. An operating leasing (long term) is a fixed obligation. This fixed obligation, although not capitalized needs to be taken into consideration in the computation of earnings to fixed charges.

Net Interest Bearing Debt Ratio:

The Net Interest Bearing Debt Ratio compares the Net Interest Bearing Liabilities and the Net Interest Bearing Assets. It is calculated as follows;

Interest Bearing Liabilities

Interest Bearing Assets

The Net Interest Bearing Debt Ratio gives an idea about the Interest Bearing Liabilities as well as the Interest Bearing Assets. Care has to be taken to ensure that when calculating the ratio, it is specified which assets as well as liabilities are interest bearing and included in the calculation. At times, there may be some long term receivables as well as pension provisions that could be interest bearing.

Fixed Charge Coverage Ratio:

The Fixed Charge Coverage Ratio is also known as Earnings to Fixed Charges Ratio. This ratio addresses the criticism of the Interest Coverage Ratio in that it includes all fixed charges including the operating lease obligations. It is calculated as follows:

Earnings Before Fixed Charges and Taxes

Fixed Charges

Since the Fixed Charge Coverage Ratio measures the ability of Earnings Before Fixed Charges and Taxes to cover payment of all fixed charges, a ratio on the higher side is considered good.

Earnings before Fixed Charges is calculated by calculating EBIT (Earnings Before Interest and Taxes) and adding back the operating lease payments that have been expensed. The calculation of Earnings Before Fixed Charges and Taxes is shown as follows:

EBIT (Earnings Before Interest and Taxes)
+ Add back of operating lease payments that have been expensed

= Earnings Before Fixed Charges and Taxes

Fixed Charges can be calculated by adding Interest expense on capital leases and loans, Principal payments on capital leases and loans and Payments on operating leases. The calculation of Fixed Charges is shown as follows:

> Interest expense on capital leases and loans
> + Principal payments on capital leases and loans
> + Payments on operating leases
> = Total Fixed Charges

Cash Flow to Fixed Charges Ratio:

The Fixed Charges Coverage Ratio can be altered to change the numerator to Cash Flow instead of Earnings before Fixed Charges. It is calculated as follows:

$$\frac{\text{Adjusted Operating Cash Flow}}{\text{Fixed Charges}}$$

A Cash Flow to Fixed Charges Ratio on the higher side is desirable as it measures the Cash Flow available to cover Fixed Charges. Cash available to cover fixed charges is a positive sign with respect to the ability to meet obligations.

Cash Flow from Operations can be added to Fixed Charges and Tax payments to calculate Adjusted Operating Cash Flow. The calculation of Adjusted Operating Cash Flow is as follows:

> Cash flow from operations (from the Statement of Cash Flows)
> + Fixed Charges
> + Tax Payments (cash amount paid and can be found in the Statement of
Cash Flows)
> = Adjusted Operating Cash Flow

Fixed Charges in the Cash Flow to Fixed Charges Ratio are not the same as the Fixed Charges in the Fixed Charges Coverage Ratio. Fixed Charges that reduce operating cash flow are added back while those that do not reduce operating cash flow are not to be added back. Fixed charges that should be added back are interest paid on capital leases and loans, operating lease payments, taxes paid in cash as they decrease operating cash flow. Principal payments on capital leases and loans do not decrease operating cash flow as they form part of financing activities and hence are not to be added back to the operating cash flow. The calculation of Fixed Charges is as follows:

Interest expense on capital leases and loans
+Principal payments on capital leases and loans
+Payments on operating leases
= Total Fixed Charges

Effective Tax Rate:

The Effective Tax Rate compares the income tax expense and the pre tax return. It is calculated as follows:

$$\frac{\text{Income Tax Rate}}{\text{Pre Tax Income}}$$

The Effective Tax Rate will greatly affect the Net Income Available to shareholders (IACS). In case the Net Income Available to shareholders (IACS) is high and the Effective Tax Rate is low, it is considered to be a positive ratio from the point of view of the shareholders. However, care has to be taken to ensure that tax is not avoided or maneuvered (even though the maneuvering may not be illegal).

The Effective Tax Rate can differ for an organization operating in a single jurisdiction from year to year as tax rates are subject to change from year to year, depending on government policy.

A stable Effective Rate of Tax can be said to imply an organization which takes responsibility for its operations and profits rather than generating profits through avoidance or maneuvering of tax.

The Effective Tax Rate can differ as the organizations operate in different jurisdictions. The local, state and national tax rates may differ and hence different organizations within the same industry may have different Effective Tax Rate.

The Effective Tax Rate assumes special importance from the point of view of multinational organizations as multinational corporations operate in multiple jurisdictions and arte subjected to different rates of taxation and the objective is to minimize the tax expense. Many organizations, whether local (operating in a single country) or multinational, employ methods to reduce the tax burden.

Operating Self Sufficiency Ratio:

The Operating Self Sufficiency Ratio compares the Total Revenue to the Total Expenses. It is calculated as follows;

$$\frac{\text{Total Revenue}}{\text{Total Expenses}}$$

Total Revenue should exclude revenues that are not generated from ordinary operations. Total Expenses includes all expenses including social costs.

The Operating Self Sufficiency Ratio gives an idea about the ability of the revenue to cover the expenses of the organization without need for outside financing.

An Operating Self Sufficiency Ratio of 1 times or 1:1 usually means that funding from outside sources is not required. A high Operating Self Sufficiency Ratio is desirable as it indicates a higher ability of the revenue to cover expenses without the need for outside financing. On the other hand, a low Operating Self Sufficiency Ratio is not desirable as it indicates a lower ability of the revenue to cover expenses without the need for outside financing. An extremely low Operating Self Sufficiency Ratio could indicate a need for outside financing. In case the ratio is low over a period of time, the organization may face cash crunch, need for outside financing, inability to repay obligations and may lead to insolvency.

Operating Ratio:

The Operating Ratio gives an idea about the profitability of an organization through the ratio of operating expenses. It is calculated as follows:

$$\frac{\text{Cost of Goods Sold} + \text{Operating Expenses}}{\text{Net Sales}}$$

Cost of Goods Sold is calculated as follows:

Opening Stock + Purchases + Carriage + Wages + Other Direct Expenses - Closing Stock

Operating Expenses are calculated as follows:

Office and Administration Exp. + Selling and Distribution Exp. + Discount + Bad Debts + Interest on Short- term loans.

Operating Ratio gives an indication as to the amount generated from sales that is spent on cost of goods sold as well as operating expenses. Operating Ratio gives an indication as to efficiency (the amount spent on Operating Expenses whether it is high or low) as well as profitability (the amount that remains after operating expenses are paid).

A high Operating Ratio indicates that the operating expenses are high and thus the profitability will be comparatively lower. This would mean that there would be less amount available to fulfill other obligations such as interest, dividend for the shareholders as well as other corporate requirements.

On the other hand, a low Operating Ratio indicates that the operating expenses are low or within limits and thus the profitability will be comparatively higher. This would mean that there would be more amount available to fulfill other obligations such as interest, dividend for the shareholders as well as other corporate requirements.

Expenses Ratio:

The Expenses Ratio compares the Expenses to Sales or Revenue. It is calculated as follows;

$$\frac{\text{Expenses}}{\text{Sales (Revenue)}}$$

The Operating Ratio gives an idea about the Total Operating Expenses to Sales (Revenue). The Expenses Ratio takes into account the individual expenses and compares them to Sales thus giving an idea about the proportion of each expense as well as its increasing and decreasing trend (by comparing it over a period of time, comparison with competitors and industry as well as benchmark), reasons for deviation from norm as well as operating efficiency (in case Expense Ratio is well within limits) or corrective action (in case the Expense Ratio) is greater than expected).

Various Expense Ratios may be calculated such as;

$$\text{Material Consumed Ratio} = \frac{\text{Material Consumed}}{\text{Net Sales}} * 100$$

$$\text{Direct Labor Cost Ratio} = \frac{\text{Direct Labor Cost}}{\text{Net sales}} * 100$$

$$\text{Factory Expenses Ratio} = \frac{\text{Factory Expenses}}{\text{Net Sales}} * 100$$

The Material Consumed Ratio, Direct Labor Cost Ratio, Factory Expenses Ratio together will be referred to as the Cost of Goods Sold ratio.

Cost of Goods Sold Ratio is calculated as follows:

$$\text{Cost of Goods Sold Ratio} = \frac{\text{Cost of Goods Sold}}{\text{Net Sales}} * 100$$

Office and Administrative Expenses Ratio = Office and Administrative Expenses * 100

Net Sales

Selling Expenses Ratio = Selling Expenses *100

Net Sales

Non- Operating Expenses Ratio = Non-Operating Expenses *100

Net sales

REFERENCES:
1)http://pages.stern.nyu.edu/~%20adamodar/New_Home_Page/AccPrimer/inventory.htm
2)Irvin N. Gleim, Dale L. Flesher(2012) – Financial Planning, Performance and Control (Part 1), Gleim CMA Review, Sixteenth Edition.
3)Irvin N. Gleim, Dale L. Flesher(2012) – Financial Decision Making (Part 2), Gleim CMA Review, Sixteenth Edition.
4)Brian Hock, Lynn Roden, David Fairchild (2010) – Part 2 Financial Decision Making, Hock International.
5)Saurav Dutta, Tony Griffin, Karen L. Jett, Jan Kooiman, Lon Petro, Siaw-Peng Wan (2009) – CMA Learning System Part 2: Financial Decision Making, Version 3.0, Institute of Management Accountants (IMA).
6)Risk Management Association (2011) – Annual Statement Studies Financial Ratio Benchmarks 2011 2012 (www.rmahq.org).
7)Standards for the Calculation of Financial Ratios (2004)- The Danish Society of Financial Analysts, The Norwegian Society of Financial Analysts.
8)http://www.accountingcycle.org/Operating-Cycle.html
9)P Muralidhar (nd) – Ratio Analysis, Matrusri Institute of PG Studies, http://www.slideshare.net/Dharan178/ratio-analysis-2970642
10)http://www.qfinance.com/cash-flow-management-calculations/liquidity-ratio-analysis
11)http://www.allprojectreports.com/MBA-Projects/Finance-Project-Report/ratio-analysis/ratio-analysis-advantage-limitations-classification-financial-ratio-analysis.htm
12)http://www.demonstratingvalue.org/resources/financial-ratio-analysis
13)http://www3.nd.edu/~mgrecon/simulations/micromaticweb/financialratios.html
14)http://www.cliffsnotes.com/more-subjects/accounting/accounting-principles-ii/financial-statement-analysis/ratio-analysis
15)http://www.bized.co.uk/compfact/ratios/liquid1.htm
16)http://www.demonstratingvalue.org/resources/financial-ratio-analysis#Leverage
17)http://www.demonstratingvalue.org/resources/financial-ratio-analysis#Profitability
18)http://www.bized.co.uk/compfact/ratios/investor10.htm
19)http://en.wikibooks.org/wiki/AQA_Business_Studies/Ratio_Analysis
20)http://www.prenhall.com/divisions/bp/app/cfl/RA/MarketValueRatios.html
21)http://www.prenhall.com/divisions/bp/app/cfl/RA/DebtManagementRatios.html

22)http://www.investopedia.com/terms/s/shareholdersequity.asp
23)http://www.bized.co.uk/compfact/ratios/asset5.htm
24)Hemant R. Dani (2000) – Balance Sheets Content, Analysis and Interpretation, Vision Books Pvt Ltd.

SOLVENCY OR CAPITAL STRUCTURE RATIOS

Capital Structure or Solvency Ratios give an idea about the ability of an organization to repay long term or non current obligations as and when they become due. Repayment of long term or non current ability implies the ability of an organization to stay in business. Inability to repay obligations could mean default and over a period of time, it could lead to insolvency. The organization is said to be solvent when the Assets exceed the Liabilities.

The Capital Structure of an organization includes long term as well as short term sources from whom financing is obtained. The sources can be internal (equity financing) or external (debt financing). Thus, Capital Structure or Solvency ratios give an idea about the relative proportion of equity and debt in the capital structure at a given period of time.

Solvency is to be distinguished from liquidity. Solvency is the measure of the organization's ability to repay debt in the long term as and when the debt becomes due, Liquidity is the measure of cash and cash equivalents with an organization which gives an idea about the ability of an organization to fulfill its short term obligations. Liquidity therefore, will measure the ability of an organization to convert its assets into cash as most liabilities are paid in cash.

Capital Structure Ratios or Solvency Ratios include ratios such as Long Term Debt to Equity Ratio, Debt to Equity Ratio, Total Debt to Total Assets Ratio, Total Debt to Total Capital Ratio.

Solvency Ratio:

The Solvency Ratio compares the Total Assets to the Total Liabilities. It is calculated as follows:

$$\frac{\text{Total Assets}}{\text{Total Liabilities}}$$

The Solvency Ratio gives an idea whether the Total Assets of the organization are enough to cover the Total Liabilities. A high Solvency Ratio is desirable as the Total Assets would be greater than the Total Liabilities. A low Solvency Ratio on the other hand indicates that Assets may not be enough to cover Total Liabilities and may indicate a need for debt financing. A low Solvency Ratio over a period of time will be cause for concern as debt may increase and the organization may not be able to meet its obligations leading to insolvency.

Long Term Debt to Equity Ratio:

The Long Term Debt to Equity Ratio compares the Long Term Debt to Total Equity. It is calculated as follows:

$$\frac{\text{Total Debt} - \text{Current Liabilities}}{\text{Total Equity}}$$

In the Long Term Debt to Total Equity Ratio, Current Liabilities are excluded from Total Debt in order to arrive at the figure of Long Term Debt. Therefore, even in case of a Long Term Debt, the current portion of the Long Term Debt is excluded.

This ratio gives an idea about the Long Term Debt in comparison to Total Equity, giving an idea about the degree of financial leverage.

A high ratio (exceeding 1:1) indicates that Long Term Debt financing exceeds Equity financing which means that the degree of financial leverage is high. Similarly, a low ratio (lower than 1:1) indicates that Long Term Debt financing is lesser than Equity financing which means that the degree of financial leverage is low. Similarly, a ratio of 1:1 indicates equal amount of Long Term Debt financing as well as Equity financing.

A low Long Term Debt to Equity Ratio means that there is an ability to raise financing through debt. However, it also implies that the fixed costs in terms of repayments of interest and principal are lower. This also means that the Return on Capital may also be low due to not using full capacity of debt. Similarly, a high Long Term Debt to Equity Ratio means that there is little ability to raise financing through debt as the fixed costs in terms of repayments of interest and principal are higher. This also could mean that the Return on Capital may also be high due to using full capacity of debt.

Debt to Equity Ratio:

Debt to Equity Ratio compares the Debt or Liabilities to the Shareholders' Equity. It is calculated as follows:

$$\frac{\text{Total Liabilities}}{\text{Total Equity}}$$

It can also be stated as follows:

$$\frac{\text{Total Liabilities}}{\text{Shareholders' Equity}}$$

It can also be stated as follows:

$$\frac{\text{External Equities}}{\text{Internal Equities}}$$

Total Liabilities include all the liabilities of an organization whereas the Total Equity includes Shareholder Equity (preference shares included).

Since Debt to Equity Ratio compares Total Debt to Total Equity, an understanding about the source of financing is obtained. How much financing is obtained from owners (equity) and how much financing is obtained from creditors (debt) can be understood.

A high ratio (exceeding 1:1) indicates that Total Debt financing exceeds Equity financing which means that financing from creditors is high and from the owners is low. A high Debt to Equity Ratio can indicate that if additional debt is sought, it may come at unfavorable credit terms due to the high risk.

A high ratio (exceeding 1:1), especially around or above 2:1 indicates that Total Debt financing exceeds Equity financing (high leverage) which means that financing from creditors is high and from the owners is low. In such a situation, there exists a high need for calculation of other solvency or capital structure ratios. This is due to the fact that there is a moderate to high risk of default or insolvency since the repayment of the debt has to be done from profits from operations and the calculation of profitability ratios assumes importance.

Similarly, a low ratio (lower than 1:1) indicates that Total Debt financing is lesser than Equity financing which means that financing from creditors low and from the owners is high. A low Debt to Equity Ratio can indicate that additional debt can be taken for growth and expansion purposes. Similarly, a ratio of 1:1 indicates equal amount of Total Debt financing as well as Equity financing.

A low ratio indicates that Total Debt financing (low leverage) is lesser than Equity financing which means that financing from creditors low and from the owners is high. In such a situation, the need for calculation of other solvency or capital structure ratios is low. This is due to the fact that there is an extremely low risk of default or insolvency since the repayment of the debt can be easily done from profit arising from operations.

A Debt to Equity Ratio of less than 2:1 gives good assurance to long term creditors of the organization.

A limitation of the Total Debt to Total Assets Ratio is not a true measure of the debt of an organization as Total Debt includes Operational Liabilities such as Taxes Payable and Accounts Payable apart from Long Term Debt used to finance growth, investment and expansion. Operational Liabilities are used to fund the day to day operations and hence are not considered to be Leverage. Therefore, even if there is no Long Term Debt that is used to finance growth, investment and expansion, the Operational Liabilities would still be a part of the Ratio.

Total Debt to Total Capital Ratio:

Total Debt to Total Capital Ratio compares Total Debt to Total Capital. It is calculated as follows:

$$\frac{\text{Current Liabilities} + \text{Long Term Liabilities}}{\text{Total Liabilities} + \text{Total Equity}}$$

Total Capital includes Total Liabilities and Total Equity which by definition corresponds to the figure of Total Assets. Hence, in the ratio of Total Debt to Total Capital Ratio, the Total Capital corresponds to the figure of Total Assets.

The Total Debt to Total Capital Ratio includes all liabilities including Current Liabilities and Long Term Liabilities. Current Liabilities may include items such as Accounts Payable on which interest need not be paid. Hence the Total Debt to Total Capital Ratio is considered to be more conservative as compared to ratios that use only Long Term Liabilities.

The Total Debt to Total Capital Ratio gives an idea as to the Capital of the organization that is financed through debt. Thus, the Total Debt to Total Capital Ratio gives an idea about the ability to repay the debt as well as the leverage of the organization.

A high ratio indicates that financing through debt is high and hence the chances of default and insolvency tend to be high in case the ratio is high for a number of periods. A low ratio indicates that financing through debt is low and hence the chances of default and insolvency tend to be low as financing may be through equity which need not be repaid and dividends may be declared as and when possible. Compulsory periodic payments need not be made for equity financing.

However, a Total Debt to Total Capital Ratio that is extremely low could indicate that debt may be obtained cheaply for growth and expansion and this option is not being used. Highly successful companies may not require to obtain financing through debt as enough cash may be generated from the operations. A Total Debt to Total Capital Ratio that is extremely high could indicate that debt may be obtained very expensively for growth and expansion which can lead to default and insolvency in the long term, if the terms are extremely unfavorable and there are not enough profits from operations to cover debt.

From the point of view of the creditors of the organization, the Total Debt to Total Capital Ratio is preferred to be low as a low ratio indicates that commitments towards repayments are low and their debt will be repaid with a low chance of default.

Total Debt to Total Assets Ratio:

The Total Debt to Total Assets Ratio compares the Total Debt to the Total Assets. It is calculated as follows:

$$\frac{\text{Total Liabilities}}{\text{Total Assets}}$$

The Total Debt to Total Assets Ratio is also known as the Total Debt to Total Capital Ratio. The Total Debt to Total Assets Ratio gives an idea about the assets that have been financed through credit. Thus, the Total Debt to Total Assets Ratio will also give an indication as to how well the creditors are protected in case of insolvency.

A high ratio indicates that financing of through debt is high (high leverage) and hence the chances of default and insolvency tend to be high in case the ratio is high for a number of periods. A low ratio indicates that financing of assets through debt is low (low leverage) and hence the chances of default and insolvency tend to be low as financing may be through equity which need not be repaid and dividends may be declared as and when possible. Compulsory periodic payments need not be made for equity financing.

However, a Total Debt to Total Assets Ratio that is extremely low could indicate that debt may be obtained cheaply for growth and expansion and this option is not being used. Highly successful companies may not require to obtain financing through debt as enough cash may be generated from the operations. A Total Debt to Total Assets Ratio that is extremely high could indicate that debt may be obtained very expensively for growth and expansion which can lead to default and insolvency in the long term, if the terms are extremely unfavorable and there are not enough profits from operations to cover debt. Generally well established, large organizations can have a high Total Debt to Total Assets Ratio without a huge risk of default or insolvency.

From the point of view of the creditors of the organization, the Total Debt to Total Assets Ratio is preferred to be low as a low ratio indicates that commitments towards repayments are low and their debt will be repaid with a low chance of default.

A limitation of the Total Debt to Total Assets Ratio is not a true measure of the debt of an organization as Total Debt includes Operational Liabilities such as Taxes Payable and Accounts Payable apart from Long Term Debt used to finance growth, investment and expansion. Operational Liabilities are used to fund the day to day operations and hence are not considered to be Leverage. Therefore, even if there is no Long Term Debt that is used to finance growth, investment and expansion, the Operational Liabilities would still be a part of the Ratio.

Capitalization Ratio:

Capitalization Ratio compares the Long Term Debt to the Shareholders' Equity and Long Term Debt. It is calculated as follows:

Long Term Debt

Long Term Debt + Shareholders' Equity

The Capitalization Ratio gives an idea about the debt that is present in the Capital Structure of an organization. Capitalization means the total of Long Term Debt and Shareholders' Equity. The

Capitalization Ratio assumes importance as a better understanding is got about the leverage used by the organization.

No particular Capitalization Ratio is considered to be right or wrong. The Capitalization Ratio can differ with each organization depending on the strategy of the organization as well as stage of development of the organization. The Capitalization Ratio in each industry is also different depending on the circumstances in each industry.

However, generally, the Long Term Debt to Total Capital Ratio is around 0.67 : 1 or 67%. This means that the Long Term Debt should be around 67% of the Total Funds.

An appropriate Capitalization Ratio (Leverage) can make available funds to the organization for growth, expansion and investment. These extra funds can help the organization achieve greater profits that the amount that is needed to be repaid by way of interest and principal repayment. In order to get the extra funds at advantageous terms, the organization needs to have a strong record of fulfilling its commitments towards repayment of debt obligations. Otherwise, funds from outside sources may not be available or if funds are available, the terms could be unfavorable.

An organization with a high Capitalization Ratio (Leverage) could have low profitability due to repayment of debt by way of principal repayment as well as interest payments. Moreover, additional funds may not be available easily or if additional funds are available, the terms may not be favorable.

In case the economic and operating conditions for the organization are favorable, debt can be easily repaid. However, if the economic and operating conditions are not very favorable, the organization might experience difficulty in repaying the debt. And difficulties in repaying debt over a period of time could indicate risk of default and insolvency.

Invested Capital Excluding Goodwill Ratio:

Invested Capital Excluding Goodwill Ratio takes into consideration the Non Current Assets along with Net Working Capital and compares them with Operating Liabilities and Other Provisions. It is calculated as follows:

Net Working Capital + Non Current Tangible Assets + Non Current Intangible Assets

Other Provisions

Other Operating Liabilities

The Invested Capital Ratio gives an idea about the capital that has been invested in operations. Goodwill is excluded in order to understand the capital invested other than through acquisitions.

Invested Capital Including Goodwill Ratio:

The Invested Capital Including Goodwill compares the Invested Capital Excluding Goodwill along with Goodwill that has been acquired excluding amortizations with the Impairment Write Downs. It is calculated as follows:

$$\frac{\text{Invested Capital Excluding Goodwill} + \text{Goodwill Acquired excluding Amortization}}{\text{Impairment Write Downs}}$$

The Invested Capital Including Goodwill gives an idea about the capital that has been invested in operations including the acquired operations.

Proprietary Ratio:

The Proprietary Ratio compares the Shareholder's Funds to the Total Funds. It is calculated as follows;

$$\frac{\text{Shareholders' Funds}}{\text{Shareholders' Funds} + \text{Long Term Loans}}$$

It is also calculated as follows:

$$\frac{\text{Proprietary Funds}}{\text{Total Assets}}$$

It is also calculated as follows:

$$\frac{\text{Capital Employed}}{\text{Total Liabilities}}$$

The Proprietary Ratio gives an indication as to the amount of funds provided by the shareholders who are the owners of the organization. Thus, the Proprietary Ratio gives an idea about the amount of funds supplied by the owners of the organization.

Generally, the Proprietary Ratio should be 33% or 0.33 : 1 or more than that. The Ideal Proprietary Ratio is 0.5:1 or 50%.

A high Proprietary Ratio is desirable as it indicates that the organization is less reliant on external funding as a source of finance which means that the pressure to earn more Earnings to repay debt through interest payments and principal repayments is less. A high Proprietary Ratio is desirable as it indicates that the organization is less reliant on external funding as a source of finance indicates security in repayment of Long Term Loans.

A low Proprietary Ratio is not very desirable as it indicates that the organization is more reliant on external funding as a source of finance which means that more amount will be generated in terms of Earnings in order to repay the debt in the form of interest payments and principal repayment. A low Proprietary Ratio is desirable as it indicates that the organization is less reliant on external funding as a source of finance also indicates that Long Term Loans are less secure in terms of repayment.

REFERENCES:

1)http://pages.stern.nyu.edu/~%20adamodar/New_Home_Page/AccPrimer/inventory.htm
2)Irvin N. Gleim, Dale L. Flesher(2012) – Financial Planning, Performance and Control (Part 1), Gleim CMA Review, Sixteenth Edition.
3)Irvin N. Gleim, Dale L. Flesher(2012) – Financial Decision Making (Part 2), Gleim CMA Review, Sixteenth Edition.
4)Brian Hock, Lynn Roden, David Fairchild (2010) – Part 2 Financial Decision Making, Hock International.
5)Saurav Dutta, Tony Griffin, Karen L. Jett, Jan Kooiman, Lon Petro, Siaw-Peng Wan (2009) – CMA Learning System Part 2: Financial Decision Making, Version 3.0, Institute of Management Accountants (IMA).
6)Risk Management Association (2011) – Annual Statement Studies Financial Ratio Benchmarks 2011 2012 (www.rmahq.org).
7)Standards for the Calculation of Financial Ratios (2004)- The Danish Society of Financial Analysts, The Norwegian Society of Financial Analysts.
8)http://www.accountingcycle.org/Operating-Cycle.html
9)P Muralidhar (nd) – Ratio Analysis, Matrusri Institute of PG Studies, http://www.slideshare.net/Dharan178/ratio-analysis-2970642
10)http://www.qfinance.com/cash-flow-management-calculations/liquidity-ratio-analysis
11)http://www.allprojectreports.com/MBA-Projects/Finance-Project-Report/ratio-analysis/ratio-analysis-advantage-limitations-classification-financial-ratio-analysis.htm
12)http://www.demonstratingvalue.org/resources/financial-ratio-analysis
13)http://www3.nd.edu/~mgrecon/simulations/micromaticweb/financialratios.html
14)http://www.cliffsnotes.com/more-subjects/accounting/accounting-principles-ii/financial-statement-analysis/ratio-analysis
15)http://www.bized.co.uk/compfact/ratios/liquid1.htm
16)http://www.demonstratingvalue.org/resources/financial-ratio-analysis#Leverage
17)http://www.demonstratingvalue.org/resources/financial-ratio-analysis#Profitability
18)http://www.bized.co.uk/compfact/ratios/investor10.htm
19)http://en.wikibooks.org/wiki/AQA_Business_Studies/Ratio_Analysis
20)http://www.prenhall.com/divisions/bp/app/cfl/RA/MarketValueRatios.html
21)http://www.prenhall.com/divisions/bp/app/cfl/RA/DebtManagementRatios.html
22)http://www.investopedia.com/terms/s/shareholdersequity.asp
23)http://www.bized.co.uk/compfact/ratios/asset5.htm
24)Hemant R. Dani (2000) – Balance Sheets Content, Analysis and Interpretation, Vision Books Pvt Ltd.

ACTIVITY RATIOS

Activity ratios help evaluate whether the management of resources is efficient or not including current assets (inventory and accounts receivable). Accounts Receivable Turnover Ratio, Inventory Turnover Ratio, Accounts Payable Turnover Ratio, Total Asset Turnover Ratio, Fixed Asset Turnover Ratio are some of the various Activity Ratios.

Total Asset Turnover Ratio:

Total Asset Turnover Ratio measures sales (total revenue) in relation to total assets. It is calculated as follows:

$$\frac{\text{Sales}}{\text{(Average) Total Assets}}$$

Average Total Assets are calculated as follows:

$$\frac{\text{Beginning Fixed Assets + Ending Fixed Assets}}{2}$$

Some formulae use year end balances instead of Average Balances. When financial statements of multiple periods are available, average balances may be uses. In case information of a single period is available, year end balance may be used. This usually depends upon preference of the analyst.

Total Asset Turnover Ratio can be considered to be an overall activity ratio. This ratio helps understand the revenue that that assets are generating. It shows how efficiently the investments of short term Assets as well as long term assets are being used in order to generate revenue and sales.

The Total Assets Turnover Ratio is to be used in conjunction with operating ratios to determine the efficiency in the use of assets. Moreover, organizations within the same industry may be compared with ease while organizations in different industries may be difficult to compare in terms of the Total Assets Turnover Ratio.

There is no particular ideal Total Asset Turnover Ratio. However, a ratio of 2 times is generally considered good.

Fixed Asset Turnover Ratio:

Fixed Asset Turnover Ratio measures sales (total revenue) in relation to fixed assets. It is calculated as follows:

$$\frac{\text{Sales}}{\text{(Average) Fixed Assets}}$$

Average Fixed Assets can be calculated as follows:

$$\frac{\text{Beginning Fixed Assets} + \text{Ending Fixed Assets}}{2}$$

Some formulae use year end balances instead of Average Balances. When financial statements of multiple periods are available, average balances may be uses. In case information of a single period is available, year end balance may be used. This usually depends upon preference of the analyst.

Fixed Assets are Plant, Equipment and Property. The Fixed Assets Turnover Ratio is a part of Total Asset Turnover Ratio. In the Total Assets Turnover Ratio, all assets (fixed assets, long term assets as well current assets, are taken into consideration, Fixed Asset Turnover Ratio only takes into consideration the fixed assets ignoring current assets.

Depreciation and the method used to calculate depreciation (Straight Line Method, Declining Balance Method, Annuity Depreciation, Sum of Digits Method, Units of Production Method, Units of Time Method, Group Depreciation Method, Composite Depreciation Method) will affect the Fixed Assets Turnover Ratio. In case depreciation calculate is a large figure or in case of an organization which is labor intensive, the Fixed Asset Turnover Ratio may be distorted.

The Fixed Asset Turnover Ratio gives an indication as to how the Capital invested in Fixed Assets is used. However, there is no ideal Fixed Asset Turnover Ratio. However a ratio of 5 times is usually considered a good ratio. Hence, the Fixed Asset Turnover Ratio has to be compared to prior periods in order to determine efficiency in use of assets. If the Fixed Asset Turnover Ratio shows a rising or a stable trend, it indicates that there is efficient use of assets which indicates efficient use of capital investment in fixed assets. However, a declining Fixed Asset Turnover Ratio is a cause for concern as assets as not being put to efficient use and capital investment in assets is not being utilized appropriately.

Care has to be taken to compare organizations within the same industry and organizations in the same industry of a similar size otherwise the comparison will not yield fruitful results as the assets of the two organizations may differ in nature as well as size.

Current Asset Turnover Ratio:

The Current Asset Turnover Ratio compares sales (total revenue) to the current assets. It is calculated as follows:

$$\frac{\text{Sales}}{\text{(Average) Current Assets}}$$

Average Fixed Assets can be calculated as follows:

$$\frac{\text{Beginning Fixed Assets + Ending Fixed Assets}}{2}$$

Some formulae use year end balances instead of Average Balances. When financial statements of multiple periods are available, average balances may be uses. In case information of a single period is available, year end balance may be used. This usually depends upon preference of the analyst.

Current Assets are assets that can be converted into cash or consumed or sold within a short period of time (usually the longer period between a year or an operating cycle). Thus, liquidity ratios generally give an idea about the ability of an organization to carry out its operations in the short run.

Current Assets include Cash and Cash Equivalents, Accounts Receivable, Prepaid Items, Inventory, Marketable Securities.

Fixed Assets to Capital Employed Ratio:

The Fixed Assets to Capital Employed Ratio compares the Fixed Assets and the Capital Employed. It is calculated as follows:

$$\frac{\text{Fixed Assets}}{\text{Capital Employed}}$$

The Fixed Assets to Capital Employed Ratio gives an idea about the financing of the Fixed Assets through the Capital Employed (long term funds as well as short term funds) in the organization.

A good Fixed Assets to Capital Employed Ratio is considered to be 0.67 : 1 or 0.67 times. However, the Fixed Assets to Capital Employed Ratio should ideally not be more than 1: 1 or 1.

Fixed Assets to Proprietors Funds (Net Worth) Ratio:

The Fixed Assets to Proprietors Funds (Net Worth) Ratio compares the Fixed Assets to the Proprietors Funds (Net Worth). It is calculated as follows:

Fixed Assets

Proprietors Funds (Net Worth)

Proprietors Funds are the Shareholders' Funds. Fixed Assets are Plant, Equipment and Property.

The Fixed Assets to Proprietors Funds (Net Worth) Ratio gives an indication as to the use of the Shareholders' Funds in the Fixed Assets (which have a relatively low turnover) of the organization. Usually, the Fixed Assets of the organization must be financed by the Shareholders of the organization.

A Fixed Assets to Proprietors Funds (Net Worth) Ratio of 0.75 : 1 or 0.75 times is considered a good ratio. In case the Fixed Assets to Proprietors Funds (Net Worth) Ratio is less than 100%, this indicates that the Fixed Assets have been purchased by the shareholders and the remaining amount has been put to use as Working Capital. This would indicate that dividends declared to the shareholders could be low. This could also indicate overcapitalization. However, in case the Fixed Assets to Proprietors Funds (Net Worth) Ratio is greater than 100%, it indicates that the Shareholders' Funds have not been sufficient to purchase Fixed Assets and the funding for Fixed Assets may have been done through debt (outside sources of finance).

Current Assets to Proprietors Funds (Net Worth) Ratio:

The Current Assets to Proprietors Funds (Net Worth) Ratio compares the Current Assets to Proprietors Funds (Net Worth) Ratio. It is calculated as follows;

Current Assets

Proprietors Funds (Net Worth) Ratio

The Current Assets to Proprietors Funds (Net Worth) Ratio gives an indication as to the use of the Shareholders' Funds in the Current Assets of the organization. The Current Assets to Proprietors Funds (Net Worth) Ratio instead of being a stand alone ratio has to be taken into consideration along with the Fixed Assets to Proprietors Funds (Net Worth) Ratio.

A high Current Assets to Proprietors Funds (Net Worth) Ratio in comparison to the Fixed Assets to Proprietors Funds (Net Worth) Ratio is desirable as it shows financial strength of the organization. A low Current Assets to Proprietors Funds (Net Worth) Ratio in comparison to the Fixed Assets to Proprietors Funds (Net Worth) Ratio is not very desirable as it may show financial weakness of the organization depending on the industry in which the organization operates.

Current Liabilities to Proprietors Funds (Net Worth) Ratio:

The Current Liabilities to Proprietors Funds (Net Worth) Ratio compares the Current Liabilities to the Proprietors Funds (Net Worth). It is calculated as follows:

$$\text{Current Liabilities}$$

$$\text{Proprietors Funds (Net Worth)}$$

The Current Liabilities to Proprietors Funds (Net Worth) Ratio gives an indication about the contribution of the creditors of the organization to the Capital Structure of the organization.

A Current Liabilities to Proprietors Funds (Net Worth) Ratio of 1 : 3 is considered to be good. If the Current Liabilities to Proprietors Funds (Net Worth) Ratio is high it indicates that the contribution of the creditors to the Capital Structure is high and it could also mean that credit may be difficult to obtain and if credit is obtained it could be obtained on unfavorable terms.

If the Current Liabilities to Proprietors Funds (Net Worth) Ratio is low it indicates that the contribution of the creditors to the Capital Structure is low and it could also mean that credit may be obtained it could be obtained on relatively favorable terms.

Capital Employed Turnover:

The Capital Employed Turnover Ratio compares sales (total revenue) to the shareholders' funds. It is calculated as follows:

$$\text{Sales}$$

$$\text{Equity or Common Shareholders' Funds}$$

Equity or Common Shareholders' funds are calculated as follows:

$$\text{Total Assets} - \text{Total Liabilities}$$

Equity or Common Shareholders' funds are also calculated as follows:

$$\text{Share Capital} + \text{Retained Earnings} - \text{Treasury Shares}$$

Working Capital Turnover Ratio:

The Working Capital Turnover Ratio compares sales (total revenue) to the shareholders' funds. It is calculated as follows:

$$\text{Sales}$$

$$\text{(Average) Working Capital}$$

It can also be calculated as follows:

$$\text{Cost of Sales}$$

$$\text{(Average) Working Capital}$$

Working Capital is calculated as follows:

Current Assets – Current Liabilities

Average Working Capital is calculated as follows:

Beginning Working Capital + Ending Working Capital

2

A high Working Capital Ratio is considered to be desirable as it indicates that the Working Capital is being used efficiently. However, a very high Working Capital Ratio could be undesirable as it could indicate idle Assets and hence, inefficient use of Assets. A low Working Capital Ratio is not desirable as it indicates inefficient use of Assets.

Return on Investment (ROI) Ratio:

The Return on Investment (ROI) Ratio compares the profits earned and the investments made in the assets of an organization. It is calculated as follows:

Net Income (NI)

Total Assets

The Return on Investment (ROI) Ratio may be expressed in terms of percentage. There are many ways of calculating Assets. When Average Assets are used, the formula is the same as the Return on Assets (ROA) Ratio. When Shareholder Equity is used as Total Assets in the formula, the formula is the same as the Return on Equity (ROE) Ratio.

The higher the Return on Investment (ROI) Ratio, the higher is the efficiency in which the assets are used to generate profits. An increasing Return on Investment (ROI) Ratio over a period of time shows increasing asset efficiency which is a good sign for the organization. The lower the Return on Investment (ROI) Ratio, the lower is the efficiency with which the assets are used to generate profits and hence an analysis is required as to how to improve the usage of assets in order to generate more profits. A declining Return on Investment (ROI) Ratio overtime indicates that assets are not being efficiently used and analysis as to idle assets, obsolescence etc may be necessary.

Return on Capital Employed (ROCE) Ratio:

The Return on Capital Employed (ROCE) Ratio compares the Earnings Before Interest and Taxes (EBIT) to the Capital Employed. It is calculated as follows:

Earnings Before Interest and Taxes (EBIT)

Capital Employed

Capital Employed is calculated as follows:

Equity Capital + Debt (Funded Debt)

The Return on Capital Employed (ROCE) Ratio gives a better idea about the leverage through an analysis of the debt. The Return on Capital Employed (ROCE) Ratio also gives an idea about the effect of leverage on Net Income (NI) and profitability of the organization.

The Return on Capital Employed (ROCE) Ratio is considered to be a comprehensive indicator of the profitability of an organization. The Return on Capital Employed (ROCE) Ratio also helps understand the ability of an organization to generate profits from the sources of capital that is employed by the organization.

Return on Invested Capital Excluding Goodwill Ratio:

The Return on Invested Capital Excluding Goodwill Ratio compares the Earnings Before Interest, Taxes and Amortization (EBITA) excluding Goodwill Write Downs and the Average Invested Capital Excluding Goodwill. It is calculated as follows:

Earnings Before Interest, Taxes and Amortization (EBITA) excluding Goodwill Write Downs

Average Invested Capital Excluding Goodwill

The Return on Invested Capital Excluding Goodwill Ratio gives an idea about the ability of an organization to return from its operations for the Average Capital that has been invested in the business except through acquisitions. The Return on Invested Capital Excluding Goodwill Ratio is a very good measure to analyze the performance of the operations over time as well as for analyzing the performance from operations between organizations.

Return on Invested Capital Including Goodwill Ratio:

The Return on Invested Capital Including Goodwill Ratio compares the Earnings Before Interest, Taxes and Amortization (EBITA) and the Average Invested Capital Including Goodwill. It is calculated as follows:

Earnings Before Interest, Taxes and Amortization (EBITA)

Average Invested Capital Including Goodwill

The Return on Invested Capital Including Goodwill Ratio gives a fair idea about the Earnings from all operations including acquisitions for the Average Capital that has been invested in the business including acquisitions. When the Return on Invested Capital Including Goodwill Ratio is compared to the Weighted Average Cost of Capital (WACC) taking into account and deduction of the Tax on the operations of an organization, the Return on Invested Capital Including Goodwill Ratio gives an idea about the value that is being created for the shareholders.

Sales to Invested Capital Excluding Goodwill Ratio:

The Sales to Invested Capital Excluding Goodwill Ratio compares the Net Sales and the Average Capital Invested excluding Goodwill. It is calculated as follows:

$$\frac{\text{Net Sales}}{\text{Average Capital Invested Excluding Goodwill}}$$

The Sales to Invested Capital excluding Goodwill Ratio gives a good idea about the efficiency with which the capital of the organization is employed. The Sales to Invested Capital Excluding Goodwill Ratio is extremely helpful to express the intensity of capital in the organization.

Sales to Invested Capital Including Goodwill Ratio:

The Sales to Invested Capital Including Goodwill Ratio compares the Net Sales and the Average Capital Invested including Goodwill. It is calculated as follows:

$$\frac{\text{Net Sales}}{\text{Average Capital Invested Including Goodwill}}$$

The Sales to Invested Capital Including Goodwill Ratio is a good measure of an analysis of the Return on Invested Capital (ROIC) Ratio including Goodwill.

A limitation of the Sales to Invested Capital Including Goodwill Ratio is that a comparison with prior year trends as well as comparison between organizations is not possible.

Sales to Net Working Capital Ratio:

The Sales to Net Working Capital Ratio compares the Sales and the Net Working Capital. It is calculated as follows:

$$\frac{\text{Net Sales}}{\text{Net Working Capital}}$$

Working Capital is calculated as follows:

$$\text{Current Assets} - \text{Current Liabilities}$$

The Sales to Net Working Capital gives an idea about the relationship between sales and the working capital of the organization. The Sales to Net Working Capital Ratio gives an idea if additional working capital could be needed in order to generate more revenue from sales.

Return on Total Shareholders' Funds Ratio:

The Return on Shareholders' Funds Ratio compares the Net Profit after Interests and Taxes to the Shareholders' Funds. It is calculated as follows:

Net Profit after Interests and Taxes

Total Shareholders' Funds

Total Shareholders' Funds are calculated as follows;

Equity Share Capital + Preference Share Capital + All Reserves + Balance in P&L A/c – Fictitious Assets

The Return on Shareholders' Funds Ratio gives an idea as to the usage of the Shareholders' Funds. The Return on Shareholders' Funds Ratio is usually compared to other similar organizations within the industry to understand the strength as well as profitability of the organization.

Return on Equity Shareholders' Funds Ratio:

The Return on Equity Shareholders' Funds Ratio compares the Net Profit after Interests, Taxes and Preference Dividend and compares it with the Equity Shareholders' Funds. It is calculated as follows:

Net Profit after Interests, Taxes and Preference Dividend

Equity Shareholders' Funds

Equity Shareholders' Funds are calculated as follows:

Equity Share Capital + All Reserves + Balance in P&L A/c – Fictitious Assets

The Return on Equity Shareholders' Funds Ratio gives an idea as to the usage of the Equity Shareholders' Funds. The Return on Equity Shareholders' Funds Ratio gives an idea about the earning capacity of the shareholders and is thus a measure of efficiency of the organization.

A high Return on Equity Shareholders' Funds Ratio is desirable as it indicates higher dividend as well as capital appreciation in the form of price rise of the shares. A low Return on Equity Shareholders' Funds Ratio is not desirable as dividends declared may be less or no dividends may be declared at all and capital appreciation in the form of rise in share price may be little to none at all.

Sales (Revenue) Per Employee Ratio:

The Sales (Revenue) Per Employee Ratio compares the Net Revenue (Sales) and the average number of employees in the organization. It is calculated as follows:

Net Sales (Revenue)

Average Number of Employees

Average number of Employees is used in the Sales (Revenue) Per Employee Ratio. This is due to the fact that the number of employees in an organization will change due to employment of new employees as well as the reduction of employees due to attrition and firing.

The Sales (Revenue) Per Employee Ratio gives an idea about the Net Revenue generated per employee. Thus, the Sales (Revenue) Per Employee Ratio gives an idea about the productivity of the employees in an organization to generate sales and revenue.

A higher Sales (Revenue) Per Employee Ratio is preferred as this means that the employees are highly productive whereas a low Sales (Revenue) Per Employee Ratio indicates low productivity of the employees.

The Sales (Revenue) Per Employee Ratio is essentially an internal ratio to the organization for the purposes of measuring efficiency and productivity. Individuals and organizations that are not part of the organization do not usually calculate this ratio as it would not only be difficult to obtain data on employees but also because it does not affect the decisions made regarding the organization.

Earnings Per Employee Ratio:

The Earnings Per Employee Ratio compares the Net Income (NI) and the average number of employees in the organization. It is calculated as follows:

Net Income (NI)

Average Number of Employees

Average number of Employees is used in the Sales (Revenue) Per Employee Ratio. This is due to the fact that the number of employees in an organization will change due to employment of new employees as well as the reduction of employees due to attrition and firing.

The Earnings Per Employee Ratio gives an idea about the Net Income (NI) or profits generated per employee. Thus, the Earnings Per Employee Ratio gives an idea about the productivity of the employees in an organization in generating profits for the organization.

A Earnings Per Employee Ratio is preferred as this means that the employees are highly productive whereas a low Earnings Per Employee Ratio indicates low productivity of the employees.

The Earnings Per Employee Ratio is essentially an internal ratio to the organization for the purposes of measuring efficiency and productivity. Individuals and organizations that are not part of the organization do not usually calculate this ratio as it would not only be difficult to obtain data on employees but also because it does not affect the decisions made regarding the organization.

Earnings Before Interest, Taxes and Amortization (EBITA) Per Employee Ratio:

The Earnings Before Interest, Taxes and Amortization (EBITA) Per Employee Ratio compares the Earnings Before Interest, Taxes and Amortization (EBITA) to the Average Employees in the organization. It is calculated as follows:

Earnings Before Interest, Taxes and Amortization (EBITA)

Average Number of Employees

Average number of Employees is used in the Sales (Revenue) Per Employee Ratio. This is due to the fact that the number of employees in an organization will change due to employment of new employees as well as the reduction of employees due to attrition and firing.

The Earnings Before Interest, Taxes and Amortization (EBITA) Per Employee Ratio gives an idea about the Operating Profit that is generated per employee. Thus, the Earnings Before Interest, Taxes and Amortization (EBITA) Per Employee Ratio gives an idea about the productivity of the employees in an organization in generating profits for the organization.

A higher Earnings Before Interest, Taxes and Amortization (EBITA) Per Employee Ratio is preferred as this means that the employees are highly productive whereas a low Earnings Before Interest, Taxes and Amortization (EBITA) Per Employee Ratio indicates low productivity of the employees.

The Earnings Before Interest, Taxes and Amortization (EBITA) Per Employee Ratio is essentially an internal ratio to the organization for the purposes of measuring efficiency and productivity. Individuals and organizations that are not part of the organization do not usually calculate this ratio as it would not only be difficult to obtain data on employees but also because it does not affect the decisions made regarding the organization.

Return on Assets (ROA) Ratio:

The Return on Assets (ROA) Ratio compares Net Income (NI) to Total Assets. Return on Assets Ratio can be calculated as follows:

Net Income

(Average) Total Assets

It can also be calculated as follows:

$$\frac{\text{Earnings Before Interest and Taxes (EBIT)}}{\text{(Average) Total Assets}}$$

Average Total Assets are calculated as follows:

$$\frac{\text{Beginning Total Assets + Ending Total Assets}}{2}$$

Some formulae use year end balances instead of Average Balances. When financial statements of multiple periods are available, average balances may be uses. In case information of a single period is available, year end balance may be used. This usually depends upon preference of the analyst.

Some analysts use Earnings Before Interest and Taxes (EBIT). This is due to the fact that the earnings are sought to be matched to the use of the assets by the Operating managers. Assets do not directly pay interests and taxes. The amount generated from assets can be used for operating purposes first and any remaining amount can then go towards payments of interest and taxes. Thus, payments towards interest and taxes are an indirect use of assets.

Operating managers do not generally decide on payments of taxes and interest. Such decisions are usually made by the Senior Managers. The Return on Assets (ROA) Ratio is generally calculated to determine efficiency in use of assets by the operating managers. Since operating managers do not control the amount of interest and taxes that are to be paid, they should not be held responsible for them.

The Return on Assets (ROA) ratio is a very popular measure that gives an indication about the efficiency in the use of assets as well as the overall profitability of the organization. Along with the Return on Equity (ROE) Ratio, the Return on Assets (ROA) Ratio is widely used in rankings of organizations from a same or a similar industry. An ideal Return on Assets (ROA) Ratio is not less than 5% although there are significant exceptions to this ideal standard.

A high Return on Assets (ROA) Ratio is indicative of a successful organization that uses the assets efficiently whereas a low Return on Assets (ROA) Ratio indicates that the organization is not doing well and that the assets are not being used efficiently and reasons for the bad performance need to be investigated.

When the same assets are able to generate income, the Return on Assets (ROA) ratio increases whereas when assets remain the same and income declines, the Return on Assets (ROA) Ratio declines.

The Return on Assets (ROA) Ratio is to be compared with the Return on Assets (ROA) Ratios of previous years. If the Return on Assets (ROA) Ratio is to be compared with that of other organizations, it is to be ensured that the organization is not only within the same industry but also of a similar size. Organizations within the same industry may be of different sizes and therefore the amount as well as value of their assets may differ and hence the Return on Assets (ROA) Ratio may differ substantially.

Inventory Turnover Ratio:

The Inventory Turnover Ratio makes a connection between Inventory and Cost of Goods Sold. It i s calculated as follows:

$$\frac{\text{Annual Cost of Goods Sold}}{\text{Average Inventory}}$$

Average Inventory is calculated as follows:

$$\frac{\text{Beginning Inventory + Ending Inventory}}{2}$$

Some formulae use year end balances instead of Average Balances. When financial statements of multiple periods are available, average balances may be uses. In case information of a single period is available, year end balance may be used. This usually depends upon preference of the analyst.

If level of fluctuation in Inventory is high eg. Seasonally there is fluctuation in Inventory, inventory can be calculated using actual monthly balances.

Cost of Sales needs to be annualized. In case the period of one quarter is being considered, the figure should be multiplied by 4, in case the period of two quarters is being considered, the figure should be multiplied by 2 and so on.

The only care that needs to be taken is to ensure that the same period is reflected in both, the numerator and the denominator.

The Inventory Turnover Ratio gives a fair idea about the salability of the inventory. It calculates the ability of the company to sell the inventory. It answers the question of how many times the inventory is sold during a specified period, usually a year. The ideal Inventory Turnover Ratio is 8 times. A high ratio is desirable as it indicates that Inventory is being sold at a fast rate and maintenance of unmarketable and obsolete inventories is at a low level. However, care must be taken to ensure that adequate inventory is maintained as sales may be lost if inventory is too low.

Increase in Cost of Goods sold but no increase in Inventory level or decrease in inventory level indicates a high turnover level. It means that as inventory is sold, the cost of sale is included in the cost of goods sold. It indicates good inventory management. In case the ratio is excessively high, it may also mean that not enough inventory is being maintained and sales could be lost as there is not enough stock to be sold.

A decrease in Inventory Turnover Ratio could be a result of increase in inventory with no change in cost of goods sold or decrease in cost of goods sold could mean that inventory is being sold slowly and could also mean that too much inventory is being held (maybe unmarketable or obsolete). On the other hand, inventory may have been maintained at a high level on purpose in order to avoid shortage of inventory for sale. Risk of losing out on sales due to low stocks is low. However, the risk of losing better investment opportunities due to high level of inventory is high. However, in case of build up of inventory, there may be expectation that sales may pick up at a later date and although Inventory Turnover Ratio is low at a particular time, as sales pick up the ratio may adjust. However, a low Inventory Turnover Ratio for a prolonged period is always a sign of concern.

Care must be taken to take into consideration the seasonal fluctuations in inventory as there are industries in which there are a lot of fluctuations in sales due to seasonality due to the nature of their products. The period for which the Inventory Turnover Ratio is calculated needs to be taken into consideration for interpretation of the Inventory Turnover Ratio.

In case the level of Inventory is zero, the quotient will be undefined as the denominator will be zero. The Inventory Turnover Ratio is optimum when the Inventory Turnover Ratio is undefined as this indicates that inventory will be zero. In a Lean (Just in Time) system, the aim is to have little to no inventory to avoid holding costs and to reduce Total Costs and deliver value to the customer by reducing cost while increasing quality of the products.

Since the denominator is the Inventory that is maintained, keeping a low level of Inventory will result in a high Inventory Turnover Ratio. On the other hand, if the Inventory Turnover Ratio is low, it could be because the inventory maintained is high.

The Inventory Turnover Ratio can range from very high to very low, including undefined. An Inventory Turnover Ratio can be zero or close to zero when inventory is more than the Cost of Goods Sold (COGS).

Choice of the method of calculation of inventory (FIFO (First In First Out), LIFO (Last In First Out) etc) and Weighted Average Method will affect the valuation of Inventory. In order to understand this ratio better, the method of inventory valuation have to be considered. Companies that use different methods of valuation, even in the same industry will be difficult to compare with each other.

Different industries will have different ideal Inventory Turnover Ratios. Non durable items require a high Inventory Turnover Ratio whereas durable items could have a comparatively low Inventory Turnover Ratio. Items like milk, meat and other edible items therefore require a high Inventory Turnover Ratio whereas durable items such as furniture, jewellery etc can have a comparatively low Inventory Turnover Ratio. Service Industries may not have an Inventory Turnover Ratio.

With the current trend towards Just – in – Time and Lean Systems, more and more organizations are aiming towards keeping little to no inventory in order to avoid carrying costs (inventory storage costs) as well as decay and loss from natural factors as well as theft and obsolescence.

Inventory Turnover Ratio (In Days):

The Inventory Turnover Ratio in days is much like the Inventory Turnover Ratio. The only difference is that the Inventory Turnover Ratio calculates how many times a year the inventory is sold whereas the Inventory Turnover Ratio in days calculates the number of days it takes for inventory to be sold and turned into cash. It is calculated as follows:

$$\frac{365, \ 360 \ or \ 300}{Inventory \ Turnover}$$

It can also be calculated as follows:

$$\frac{Average \ Inventory}{Average \ Daily \ Cost \ of \ Sales}$$

It can also be calculated as follows:

$$\frac{Annual \ Cost \ of \ Goods \ Sold}{Average \ Inventory} * (365 \ or \ 360 \ or \ 300)$$

Average Daily Cost of Sales is calculated as follows:

$$\frac{Annual \ Cost \ of \ Sales}{365, \ 360 \ or \ 300}$$

Some formulae use year end balances instead of Average Balances. When financial statements of multiple periods are available, average balances may be used. In case information of a single period is available, year end balance may be used. This usually depends upon preference of the analyst.

Calculation by either method will result in the same answer. Actual number of days in a year (365) can be used. Bankers prefer to use 360 days. This could be used. Average business days in a year are considered to be 300. This figure can be used for calculation.

Inventory to Net Working Capital Ratio:

The Inventory to Net Working Capital Ratio compares Inventory to the Net Working Capital. It is calculated as follows:

Inventory

Net Working Capital

Net Working Capital is calculated as follows:

Current Assets – Current Liabilities

The Inventory to Net Working Capital Ratio is to read in association with the Inventory Turnover Ratio.

Accounts Receivable Turnover Ratio:

Accounts Turnover Ratio makes a connection between Sales (Credit Sales) and Accounts Receivable. It i s calculated as follows:

Net Annual Credit Sales

(Average) Accounts Receivable

Average Accounts Receivable is calculated as follows:

Beginning Accounts Receivable + Ending Accounts Receivable

2

Some formulae use year end balances instead of Average Balances. When financial statements of multiple periods are available, average balances may be uses. In case information of a single period is available, year end balance may be used. This usually depends upon preference of the analyst.

Gross Accounts Receivable figure is to be used if available. In case that figure is not available, Net Accounts Receivable figure (Gross Accounts Receivable less Allowance or Reserve for Doubtful Debts) can be used.

Credit Sales need to be annualized. In case the period of one quarter is being considered, the figure should be multiplied by 4, in case the period of two quarters is being considered, the figure should be multiplied by 2 and so on.

Cash Sales are ignored as when cash is received for goods sold or services rendered, no further money is to be received. It is only when money is to be received either in part or in full that Accounts Receivable is created. Hence credit sales are to be taken into account only. Credit Sales means trade receivables only i.e. credit sales from normal business activities and not receivables from unusual transactions. This means that receivables from financing activities and investment activities are not to be considered as part of Credit Sales but is only to be included if consumer financing is part of normal business activities. In case cash sales are includes, there could be an overstatement of liquidity of the organization.

This ratio takes into consideration how many times in a specified period (usually a year), the Accounts Receivable are being turned over i.e. being converted into cash. This ratio indicates how much investment has been made in Accounts Receivable and also the efficiency of the collection policy. The ideal Accounts Receivable Turnover Ratio is 10 times to 12 times. A high ratio indicates that Accounts receivable are being collected at a faster rate and cash is being generated rapidly. A low ratio indicates that Accounts Receivable are being collected at a slower rate and cash is being generated slowly. If Accounts Receivable are zero, the Accounts Receivable Ratio is considered the best even though the Quotient is undefined as the denominator is zero. Thus, the Accounts Receivable ratio can range from a high numerical value to a lowest numerical value and even undefined. The Accounts Receivable Ratio can be zero when the Credit Sales are extremely low and the Accounts Receivable are greater than Credit Sales. However, the Accounts Receivable Ratio cannot be negative.

Comparison of this ratio over a period of time will help evaluate the company's collection rate as well as efficiency or otherwise of the collection policy. If the ratio shows an increasing trend, Accounts receivable are being collected at a faster rate and cash is being generated rapidly, indicating an efficient collection policy as well as valuable and strong customers. If the ratio shows a decreasing trend, Accounts Receivable are being collected at a slower rate and cash is being generated slowly, indicating that the collection policy is not very efficient. It could also indicate that Bad Debts may be possible leading to losses and liquidity crunch.

Credit should only be granted till the marginal profit or benefit of giving credit is either positive or zero. If the benefit of extending credit exceeds the cost of giving credit, the situation is favorable. The marginal benefit of giving credit being zero indicates that the costs of extending credit as well as the benefits of extending credit are equal to each other. In order to calculate this, the opportunity cost in terms of foregoing other investments is to be taken into consideration. However, the cost of extending credit should not exceed the benefit of extending credit as it indicates a possible loss.

In case the organization is operating in a seasonal market where sales are seasonal (eg. I the case of an umbrella manufacturer), averaging the beginning and ending balances of Accounts Receivable is not sufficient. The balances should be the monthly average instead of the yearly average.

Accounts Receivable Turnover (In Days):

The Accounts Receivable Turnover Ratio in days is much like the Accounts Receivable Turnover Ratio. The only difference is that the Accounts Receivable Turnover Ratio calculates how many times a year the Accounts Receivable is being converted to cash whereas Accounts Receivable Turnover Ratio in days calculates the number of days it takes for Accounts Receivable to be turned into cash. It is calculated as follows:

$$\frac{365, 360 \text{ or } 300}{\text{Accounts Receivables Turnover}}$$

It is also calculated as follows:

$$\frac{\text{Average Accounts Receivable}}{\text{Average Daily Sales}}$$

It can also be calculated as follows:

$$\frac{\text{Net Annual Credit Sales} * (365 \text{ or } 360 \text{ or } 300)}{(\text{Average}) \text{ Accounts Receivable}}$$

Average Daily Sales are calculated as follows:

$$\frac{\text{Annual Credit Sales}}{365, 360 \text{ or } 300}$$

Some formulae use year end balances instead of Average Balances. When financial statements of multiple periods are available, average balances may be used. In case information of a single period is available, year end balance may be used. This usually depends upon preference of the analyst.

Calculation by either method will result in the same answer. Actual number of days in a year (365) can be used. Bankers prefer to use 360 days. This could be used. Average business days in a year are considered to be 300. This figure can be used for calculation.

Gross Accounts Receivable figure is to be used if available. In case that figure is not available, Net Accounts Receivable figure (Gross Accounts Receivable less Allowance or Reserve for Doubtful Debts) can be used.

The rate of turnover has to be compared with the credit terms of the company. The ratio should also be compared over time within the company as well as with other organizations within the same industry.

The Accounts Receivable Turnover (In Days) must not be more than the credit terms of the company. If it is more, it indicates an inefficient collection policy, poor customer base, refusal to pay (bad debt) as well as customer dissatisfaction. Delay from one or more large customers could also skew the ratio. It could also lead to short term liquidity issues. Over a long term, it could indicate bad debt issues and serious liquidity problems.

The credit terms must also be evaluated in case of a low Accounts Turnover Ratio. The ideal Accounts Receivable Turnover (In Days) is 30 days to 36 days. In case the Accounts Turnover Ratio is low, it indicates that the Accounts Receivable Turnover in Days is high. Liberal credit terms may mean that sales are sought to be increased or a new product is being launched or excess production capacity is sought to be used. A tight credit policy could indicate that customers are being lost and sales could increase but are not increasing due to the credit terms being too tight.

Provision for Doubtful Debts Ratio:

Provision for Doubtful Debts Ratio makes a connection between Accounts Receivable and Doubtful Debts. It is calculated as follows:

<u>Provision for Doubtful Accounts</u>

Gross Accounts Receivable

In this ratio, Gross Accounts Receivable is to be taken into consideration, not the Net Accounts Receivable. Doubtful Debts have to be compared with total Accounts Receivable. In the figure of

Net Accounts Receivable, Doubtful Debts are subtracted from Gross Accounts Receivable thus defeating the purpose of calculating this ratio.

This ratio aims to give an idea about the percentage of bad debt that is to be expected from the total Accounts Receivable, indicating a loss of money to the company. It is calculated in terms of percentage (%).

If Provision for Doubtful Debts is more or if this ratio is high, it indicates that Accounts Receivable are not being collected efficiently. However, if Provision for Doubtful Debts is less or if this ratio is low, it indicates that Accounts Receivable are being collected efficiently.

Accounts Payable Turnover Ratio:

Accounts Payable Turnover Ratio gives information about the number of times the payables turnover for a specified period, usually a year. It is calculated as follows:

$$\frac{\text{Annual Credit Purchases}}{\text{(Average) Accounts Payable}}$$

For the purpose of this ratio, Purchases are calculated as follows;

$$\text{Cost of sales} + \text{Ending inventory} - \text{Beginning inventory}$$

Average Accounts Payable is calculated as follows:

$$\frac{\text{Beginning Fixed Assets} + \text{Ending Fixed Assets}}{2}$$

Some formulae use year end balances instead of Average Balances. When financial statements of multiple periods are available, average balances may be used. In case information of a single period is available, the year end balance may be used. This usually depends upon preference of the analyst.

From the perspective of anyone outside the organization, the calculation of the amount of Credit Purchases is difficult. Hence, the amount of Total Purchases may be substituted for the figure of Credit Purchases.

The Accounts Payable Turnover Ratio is rather difficult to measure. This is due to the fact that the information is may not be available in the financial statements very easily. Since the numerator is annual credit purchases i.e purchases for a full year, in case the period under consideration in for less than a whole year, the credit purchases will have to be annualized. In case the period of one quarter is being considered, the figure should be multiplied by 4, in case the period of two quarters is being considered, the figure should be multiplied by 2 and so on.

In order to calculate Accounts Payable, a distinction is to be made between Accounts Payable for the purpose of Inventory and Accounts Payable for General, Selling and Administrative Expenses. This distinction is however not made very often in practice. But Accounts Payable for General, Selling and Administrative Expenses are paid promptly most of the time and are hence not very material.

Calculation of Purchases is also difficult although a rough estimate is got by applying the formula. But in case of a manufacturing company, the calculation of Inventory is very difficult. If Absorption Costing is used, all manufacturing costs, labor costs, depreciation costs, as well as all other variable costs and fixed costs will be have to be taken into account in the calculation of Cost of Goods sold and Inventory. But all these will not be reflected in Accounts Payable. Eg. Depreciation is a non cash expense and has no payable. Yet it is included in Cost of Goods Sold. Therefore, the figure of Accounts Payable needs to be adjusted for such items. And access to this information is almost restricted to analysts within the organization rather than people outside the organization, making it harder for those on the outside to calculate this ratio effectively.

The ideal Accounts Payable Turnover Ratio is 12 times. The higher the ratio the better it is for the company as it indicates that the company is paying its debts easily. A lower ratio indicates that the debts may be paid slowly and in case of a recurring low ratio, it could also indicate larger liquidity problems.

Accounts Payable Turnover Ratio (In Days):

The Accounts Payable Turnover Ratio (In Days) is much like the Accounts Payable Turnover Ratio. The only difference is that the Accounts Payable Turnover Ratio calculates how many times a year the Accounts Payable is being paid in cash whereas Accounts Payable Turnover Ratio in days calculates the number of days it takes for Accounts Payable to be paid in cash. It is calculated as follows:

$$\frac{365, \ 360 \ or \ 300}{Accounts \ Payables \ Turnover}$$

It is also calculated as follows:

$$\frac{Average \ Accounts \ Payable}{Average \ Daily \ Sales}$$

It can also be calculated as follows:

$$\frac{\text{Average Accounts Payable} * (365 \text{ or } 360 \text{ or } 300)}{\text{Credit Purchases}}$$

Average Daily Sales are calculated as follows:

$$\frac{\text{Annual Credit Purchases}}{365, 360 \text{ or } 300}$$

Some formulae use year end balances instead of Average Balances. When financial statements of multiple periods are available, average balances may be uses. In case information of a single period is available, year end balance may be used. This usually depends upon preference of the analyst.

Calculation by either method will result in the same answer. Actual number of days in a year (365) can be used. Bankers prefer to use 360 days. This could be used. Average business days in a year are considered to be 300. This figure can be used for calculation.

From the perspective of anyone outside the organization, the calculation of the amount of Credit Purchases is difficult. Hence, the amount of Total Purchases may be substituted for the figure of Credit Purchases.

Total Purchases can be calculated as follows:

Beginning Raw Material
+Purchases
+Freight Inwards
- Returns
- Ending Raw Material

The ideal Accounts Payable Turnover Ratio (In Days) is 30 days. If the Accounts Payable Turnover Ratio (In Days) ratio is low, it indicates that prompt payments are being made with regard to the payables. On the other hand, the higher the ratio, the slower it is that payment is being made of payables. It could indicate that credit terms obtained from creditors are extremely lenient and relationship with suppliers is good. It could also be indicative of liquidity issues in case the trend is continued over a long term. It could indicate a liquidity crunch and need to borrow in the short term. Over a period of time, it could indicate risk of default and even insolvency.

To analyze the Accounts Payable Turnover Ratio (in days) analysis of the terms of credit with the creditors has to be done in order to get a clearer picture of the Accounts Payable Turnover Ratio (in days). A number that is greater than the credit terms indicate would be indicative of past due obligations.

Operating Cycle:

Calculation of an Operating Cycle gives an idea as to the conversion of investments in cash in terms of Accounts Receivable and Inventory back into cash through the process of sales and collections. Operating Cycle is calculated as follows:

Accounts Receivable Turnover (In Days) + Inventory Turnover Ratio (In Days)

The Operating Cycle is extremely useful to calculate the profitability of an organization. The Operating Cycle is used along with the Cash Cycle in order to understand the liquidity position of an organization.

Cash Cycle:

Cash Cycle, also known as the Cash Conversion Cycle is the calculation of the number of days in which cash is kept in the operating cycle. It is calculated as follows:

Accounts Receivable Turnover (In Days) + Inventory Turnover Ratio (In Days) - Accounts Payable Turnover Ratio (In Days)

The Cash Cycle expresses the liquidity position of an organization through the calculation of the conversion of investments in cash in terms of Accounts Receivable and Inventory back into cash through the process of sales and collections. But the fact that certain purchases are made on credit is also taken into consideration and the payment of the credit purchases is accounted for in the calculation of the Cash Cycle.

The Cash Cycle assumes importance due to the fact that an idea is got about the efficiency of an organization in managing the Working Capital Assets. Also, the ability of an organization to repay its debt can be looked at through the Cash Cycle. Apart from the Current Ratio, Quick Ratio and Net Working Capital Ratio, the Cash Cycle gives an indication as to the liquidity of an organization.

If the Inventory Turnover Ratio (in days) is high, which means that Inventory is being turned to cash at a slower rate and the Accounts Receivable are being converted into cash at a slower rate whereas the Accounts Payable have a shorter duration, it could indicate a liquidity problem implying a need to borrow (the terms of credit may not always be favorable) and over a period of time it could indicate default as well. In case such a situation arises, analysis as to the credit terms given to debtors as well as decay or obsolescence of inventory needs to be done.

On the other hand, if the Inventory Turnover (in days) is low, which means that inventory is being turned to cash at a faster rate and the Accounts Receivable are being converted into cash at a faster rate whereas the Accounts Payable have a longer duration, it could indicate a good to strong liquidity position for the organization.

An analysis of the individual ratios may give a better idea about the trends (both positive and negative) in an organization's assets and liabilities that constitute the Working Capital. An increase in the Inventory Turnover (in days) could mean that there is a decreasing demand for the products of the organization. On the other hand, if the Inventory Turnover (in days) is low, it could mean that there is strong demand for the products of the organization.

An Accounts Receivable Turnover Ratio (in days) which is decreasing gives confidence in the ability of an organization to recover debt and could also indicate that the products of the organization are popular. It could also indicate that the organization may not have a need to borrow as well as to tighten the terms of credit for debtors.

A shorter Cash Cycle indicates a strong liquidity position which translates into a low need to borrow as well as an opportunity to pay creditors by availing of discounts by paying early. This could translate into more cash being retained by an organization for growth, investment and expansion.

On the other hand, a longer Cash Cycle indicates weak liquidity position which translates into a high need to borrow as well as loss of opportunity to pay creditors and availing of discounts by paying early. This means that payment is delayed or discounts are lost and more cash is paid for the purchases. This could translate into less or no cash being retained by an organization for growth, investment and expansion.

The Current Ratio may be used to analyze liquidity however, the Cash Cycle gives an indication of the Working Capital position of an organization.

REFERENCES:

1)http://pages.stern.nyu.edu/~%20adamodar/New_Home_Page/AccPrimer/inventory.htm
2)Irvin N. Gleim, Dale L. Flesher(2012) – Financial Planning, Performance and Control (Part 1), Gleim CMA Review, Sixteenth Edition.
3)Irvin N. Gleim, Dale L. Flesher(2012) – Financial Decision Making (Part 2), Gleim CMA Review, Sixteenth Edition.
4)Brian Hock, Lynn Roden, David Fairchild (2010) – Part 2 Financial Decision Making, Hock International.
5)Saurav Dutta, Tony Griffin, Karen L. Jett, Jan Kooiman, Lon Petro, Siaw-Peng Wan (2009) – CMA Learning System Part 2: Financial Decision Making, Version 3.0, Institute of Management Accountants (IMA).

6)Risk Management Association (2011) – Annual Statement Studies Financial Ratio Benchmarks 2011 2012 (www.rmahq.org).

7)Standards for the Calculation of Financial Ratios (2004)- The Danish Society of Financial Analysts, The Norwegian Society of Financial Analysts.

8)http://www.accountingcycle.org/Operating-Cycle.html

9)P Muralidhar (nd) – Ratio Analysis, Matrusri Institute of PG Studies, http://www.slideshare.net/Dharan178/ratio-analysis-2970642

10)http://www.qfinance.com/cash-flow-management-calculations/liquidity-ratio-analysis

11)http://www.allprojectreports.com/MBA-Projects/Finance-Project-Report/ratio-analysis/ratio-analysis-advantage-limitations-classification-financial-ratio-analysis.htm

12)http://www.demonstratingvalue.org/resources/financial-ratio-analysis

13)http://www3.nd.edu/~mgrecon/simulations/micromaticweb/financialratios.html

14)http://www.cliffsnotes.com/more-subjects/accounting/accounting-principles-ii/financial-statement-analysis/ratio-analysis

15)http://www.bized.co.uk/compfact/ratios/liquid1.htm

16)http://www.demonstratingvalue.org/resources/financial-ratio-analysis#Leverage

17)http://www.demonstratingvalue.org/resources/financial-ratio-analysis#Profitability

18)http://www.bized.co.uk/compfact/ratios/investor10.htm

19)http://en.wikibooks.org/wiki/AQA_Business_Studies/Ratio_Analysis

20)http://www.prenhall.com/divisions/bp/app/cfl/RA/MarketValueRatios.html

21)http://www.prenhall.com/divisions/bp/app/cfl/RA/DebtManagementRatios.html

22)http://www.investopedia.com/terms/s/shareholdersequity.asp

23)http://www.bized.co.uk/compfact/ratios/asset5.htm

24)Hemant R. Dani (2000) – Balance Sheets Content, Analysis and Interpretation, Vision Books Pvt Ltd.

MARKET RATIOS

Market Ratios help understand how the company is doing in the market place as compared to the actual financial position of the company. Market Ratios are important from the point of view of current investors in that the shareholders get an idea about the capital appreciation or depreciation of the shares in the market. The Market Ratios are important from the view of the potential investors as they can decide whether or not to invest in the organization. The Market Ratios are important from the point of view of the organization as they help the management to understand the reputation as well as the standing of the organization in the market.

The various types of market ratios are Book Value Per share, Price to Earnings ratio, Basic Earnings Per Share, Diluted Earnings Per Share, Price to EBITDA ratio, Market to Book ratio, Earnings Yield, Dividend Payout ratio, Dividend Yield and Shareholder Return.

Return on Equity (ROE) Ratio:

The Return on Equity (ROE) Ratio takes into consideration the Net Income (NI) along with the Shareholders' Equity. It is calculated as follows:

Net Income (NI)

Average Shareholders' Equity

The Return on Equity (ROE) Ratio is expressed as a percentage and gives an idea about the profitability of an organization by giving the shareholders an idea about the return that has been earned on the investment made by the shareholders.

A high Return on Equity (ROE) Ratio is desirable as it indicates that the return to the shareholders is high and there is efficient utilization of the investment by the shareholders. On the other hand, a low Return on Equity (ROE) Ratio is considered to be a negative sign by the shareholders as the return on the investment by the shareholders is lower and the investment by the shareholders is not being utilized efficiently.

The Return on Equity (ROE) Ratio can be compared for a trend over a period of time as well as with similar companies as well as with the industry average. Different industries can have different acceptable percentages as Return on Equity (ROE).

The Return on Equity (ROE) Ratio has its limitations. In an organization with debt exceeding equity, the equity base may be small and hence, the Return on Equity (ROE) Ratio may be high inspite of the fact that the Net Income (NI) earned is not very high. Hence, the Return on Equity (ROE) Ratio has to be interpreted in the light of the Debt to Equity Ratio.

Book Value Per Share:

Book Value Per Share takes into consideration the Total Assets along with the Total liabilities along with the securities with a claim in seniority to Equity Shares. It is calculated as follows:

Common Stockholders' Equity – Senior Claims Not on Balance Sheet

Number of Equity (Common) Shares Outstanding

Claims that have seniority to Equity Shares are usually considered to be Preference Shares. However, other claims also have seniority to Equity Shares. Such claims can include claims that are not reflected on the Balance Sheet such as arrears as to cumulative Preference Shares, other preferences as to assets that Preference Shares are entitled to as well as claims related to liquidation premiums that include any additional amounts that are required to be paid to retire or liquidate Preference Stock.

The denominator, Number of Equity (Common) Shares Outstanding represents the number of Number of Equity (Common) Shares that are reflected in the Balance Sheet. It does not represent the Weighted Average Number of Equity (Common) Shares Outstanding.

The reason for the adjustment is to calculate the amount for Number of Equity (Common) Shareholders per share in the event of liquidation of the company that they would be entitled.

There are disadvantages to calculating the Book Value Per Share as a tool for valuation. This is due to the fact that valuation of Book Value Per Share is affected by Generally Accepted Accounting Principles (GAAP) that affect the valuation measures that are used to calculate Book Value Per Share.
For Example, Generally Accepted Accounting Principles (GAAP) affect valuation through the definition of an asset pr a liability. The definition of asset or liability as per Generally Accepted Accounting Principles (GAAP) may not be in consonance with economic reality. The recording of Assets in the Balance Sheet may be at Cost or Historical Value rather than Market Value.

Depreciation affects the Book Values of the Assets. The method used in calculating depreciation along with the estimated life of the Asset affects the amount of depreciation and this in turn affects the Book Value of the Assets.

Certain Intangible Assets such as Goodwill can be difficult to calculate and measure. Their actual value may be uncertain. Assets and liabilities that are off Balance Sheet (not reflected in the Balance Sheet) such as operating leases are not included in the calculation but affect the value of the Assets and Liabilities of a company for economic purposes.

Book Value is a reflection of the accounting principles that reflect In accounting entries that include adjustments to these entries that have been recorded in the books of accounts. Some entries that are included in the books of accounts including the startup capital that was recorded during the start of the organization. Also included are the proceeds received from issue of additional shares as well as the deduction in the cost of shares that have been repurchased that are also known as Treasury Stock. Retained Earnings (Net Profit less the Dividends Paid) that are accumulated throughout the life of an organization also affect the Book Value. Other Comprehensive Income that is also recorded directly to Equity also affects the Book Value.

The Book Value of a company as well as the Book Value per Share may not match the Market Value of the company as well as the Market Value per Share. The Book Value of a company as well as the Book Value per Share may also be different than the Fair Value of the company's Net Assets.

Accounting Principles can be chosen from the various methods and principles that are accepted by the Generally Accepted Accounting Principles (GAAP). Thus it is wise to adjust Book Value before calculating Book Value Per Share. The valuation of Book Value Per Share therefore has the same limitations that are generally stated as limitations for financial statements.

Price to Earnings (P/E) Ratio:

The Price to Earnings Ratio compares the market price per share to the Earnings Per Share. It is calculated as follows:

<u>Market Price per Common Share</u>

Diluted Earnings per Share

The Price to Earnings Ratio (P/E) is the most widely quoted ratio. The Price to Earnings (P/E) Ratio is also expresses as a multiple of the Earnings Per Share (EPS). The Price to Earnings Ratio gives an idea as to the amount a shareholder has to give to buy a share when compared to the Earnings of a company. It is therefore aptly referred to a ratio that gives an idea about the earning power of the company. This ratio is of significance to the investors when choosing between alternative stocks for investment purposes.

The life cycle of a company greatly affects the Price to Earnings (P/E) Ratio. Therefore, the stage of a company in the life cycle will alter the Price to Earnings (P/E) Ratio significantly. A company in the growth stage will have a high Price to Earnings (P/E) Ratio. This is due to the fact that when the company is growing, there is an expectation that profits will grow in the future and investors rush to buy the stock in expectation of higher profits and growth leading to a higher share price. A company in the declining stages of growth will have a low Price to Earnings (P/E) Ratio. This is due to the fact that when the company has low growth, there is an expectation that profits will decline in the future and investors rush to sell the stock in expectation of lower profits leading to a lower share price.

The Price to Earnings (P/E) Ratio loses its significance when there is unusually low profit as the Price to Earnings (P/E) Ratio would be exceedingly low. The Price to Earnings (P/E) Ratio in this scenario could be of significance only if there is expectation of higher profits in the future and therefore, an increase in the Market Price Per Share in which case the Price to Earnings (P/E) Ratio could be unusually high. Similarly, when there are losses, the Price to Earnings (P/E) Ratio will lose its significance. In this case, as earnings are negative, the Price to Earnings (P/E) Ratio will be negative.

The Price to Earnings (P/E) Ratio needs to be compared to the average Price to Earnings (P/E) Ratio in the industry in which the company operates and even with the sector at large.

Market to Book Ratio:

The Market to Book Ratio establishes a relationship between the Market Price of a share and the Book Value of a share. It is calculated as follows:

<u>Market Price per Share</u>

Book Value per Share

The Book Value of a share takes into account the price of a share as entered in the books of accounts. The Market Value of a share represents the price at which the share is bought and sold on the exchange where the shares are traded. A ratio of more than 1.0 is desirable as it indicates that the market value of the share is greater than the book value. This indicates investor confidence in the company as share price is indicative of the confidence the market in general and the investors in particular have in the company.

The Market to Book Ratio will usually be more than 1.0 when high earnings in the future are expected by the market. This means that the company is viewed as a high growth company with better future prospects. A Market to Book Ratio of less than 1.0 indicates that lower earnings are expected in the future. This indicates that the market is not expecting growth for the company and is losing confidence in the company's growth prospects.

Some analysts use an Unadjusted Book Value Per Share as an index against which the Market Price of the Share is to be compared. The assumption is that for similar firms in the industry, the difference between the Market Price and the Book Value should also be roughly the same. The analyst compares this difference between the Market P rice and Book Value of the company with that of the industry.

Underpriced stocks can be found through the difference between Market Value and Adjusted Book Value of the stock. The stock may be bought if the difference between the Market Value and Adjusted Book Value of the stock is very close or the Market Value of the share is just below the Adjusted Book Value of the share. This often indicates that a merger or a takeover may be on the cards as the company may be considered to be bought in view of the lower Market Price as compared to the Book Value making it a bargain buy. If the firm's overall condition is sound, a takeover or merger attempt may be on the cards. A company with a precarious financial condition or a company on the verge of bankruptcy will also have Mark Value lower that the

Book Value. However, this is not necessarily a good target for a takeover or a merger. The financial condition therefore, is also a very important factor that needs to be taken into consideration.

Earnings Yield Ratio:

Like the Price to Earnings (P/E) Ratio, the Earnings Yield Ratio also establishes a connection between the Earnings Per Share and the Market Price of the Share. It is calculated as follows:

$$\text{Diluted Earnings Per Share (annual)}$$

$$\text{Current Market Price Per Common Share}$$

The Earnings Yield Ratio is the inverse of the Price to Earnings (P/E) Ratio. The Earnings Yield Ratio gives an indication about the power of a share at current market price to produce income for the shareholder. It indicates a return to the shareholder. The Earnings Yield Ratio gives an indication of the power of 1 unit of currency invested in common or equity stock to generate income. The Earnings Yield Ratio can also give an idea about the percentage of earnings that are distributed as dividends to the shareholders as well as the percentage of earnings that are retained for investment, growth, expansion purposes.

Dividend Yield Ratio:

The Dividend Yield Ratio compares the Annual Dividend per Common or Equity Share with the Market Price of the Share. It is calculated as follows:

$$\text{Annual Dividends Per Common Share}$$

$$\text{Current Market Price Per Share}$$

The Dividend Yield Ratio compares how much of the Market Price was returned to the investors/ shareholders in the form of dividends. Thus, based on the Current Market Price of the stock and the Current Dividend, the Dividend Yield Ratio measures the cash return to the investor/shareholder for one share in the stock of the company.

The Dividend Yield Ratio is of importance to investors seeking return from their investments. If the Dividend Payout Ratio is high, this indicates that more profits are being given out to the shareholders in the form of dividends. But this also means that the company is not looking towards growth and/or expansion plans at the present moment. If the Dividend Payout Ratio is low, this indicates that more profits are being retained by the company for either growth and/or expansion prospects. Hence the dividend yield will be low. If the retained profits are wisely invested, profits will increase and the Market Price of the share will increase as a result of increase in profits. This will result in capital appreciation or capital gain. The dividend foregone today will yield capital gains in the future.

Stocks can be growth stocks (low or no dividends declared in order to generate growth through retention and investment of profits) or income stocks (declaration of steady dividends with less emphasis on aggressive growth). The price of a stock will depend on a combination of both growth resulting in capital appreciation as well as income for the shareholders. Hence, deciding on an optimum Dividend Yield is difficult.

Dividend Payout Ratio:

Dividend Payout Ratio compares the Dividend per common or equity share paid to the Basic Earnings Per Share which can be analyzed from Income Available to Common or Equity Shareholders. It is calculated as follows:

Annual Dividend Per Common Share

Basic Earnings Per Share

It can also be calculated as follows:

Total Annual Common Dividends

Income Available to Common Shareholders

The Dividend Payout Ratio measures the proportion of Net Profit after Taxes that is paid out to the shareholders as opposed to retaining the profits in the business. A growing company may have very little or even no dividend payout as it would prefer to retain profits for the purpose of growth and expansion.

The Dividend Payout Ratio is complementary to the ratio of percentage of shareholder's equity. The difference in the Dividend Payout Ratio and the Percentage of Shareholder's Equity Ratio is that the Dividend Payout Ratio takes into account the Diluted Earnings Per Share (DEPS) and is hence a more conservative ratio than the Percentage of Shareholder's Equity Ratio.

Shareholder Return Ratio:

Shareholder Return takes into consideration the price of the share and dividends declared during the year. It is calculated as follows:

$$\frac{\text{Ending Stock Price} - \text{Beginning Stock Price} + \text{Annual Dividends Per Share}}{\text{Beginning Stock Price}}$$

The Beginning Stock Price that is deducted from the Ending Stock Price is for the purpose of calculating capital gain/loss. This along with the Annual Dividend Per Share for the period will give total returns to the shareholder. When this is compared to the Beginning Stock Price,

Price/EBITDA (Earnings Before Interest, Taxes, Depreciation and Amortization) Ratio:

Price/EBITDA (Earnings Before Interest, Taxes, Depreciation and Amortization) Ratio takes into consideration the Market Price per share and the EBITDA (Earnings Before Interest, Taxes, Depreciation and Amortization). It is calculated as follows:

$$\frac{\text{Market Price per Common Share}}{\text{EBITDA per Share}}$$

EBITDA is calculated as follows:

$$\frac{\text{EBITDA}}{\text{Number of Common Shares Outstanding}}$$

The Price/EBITDA (Earnings Before Interest, Taxes, Depreciation and Amortization) Ratio can be used to ascertain the operating profitability of an organization by excluding non operating expenses and non cash charges.

The Price/EBITDA (Earnings Before Interest, Taxes, Depreciation and Amortization) Ratio is a variation of the P/E (Price to Earnings) Ratio. This is due to the fact that the Earnings Per Share used in the calculation of the ratio is EBITDA (Earnings Before Interest, Taxes, Depreciation and Amortization). The Diluted Earnings Per Share is not used to calculate this ratio.

However, using this ratio can be a little controversial. In case of a company that is not operating profitably, its P/E (Price to Earnings) Ratio is negative. The P/E (Price to Earnings) Ratio therefore becomes meaningless. However, when non operating expenses and non cash charges are excluded, the Price/EBITDA (Earnings Before Interest, Taxes, Depreciation and Amortization) Ratio could turn positive. But the only point to be considered is that EBITDA (Earnings Before Interest, Taxes, Depreciation and Amortization) can only be used for the short term. In the long term, real earnings must be seen and in such a case, EBITDA (Earnings Before Interest, Taxes, Depreciation and Amortization) is not a good measure of actual earnings.

Dividend Per Share Ratio:

The Dividend Per Share Ratio takes into account the Total Dividend and compares it with the number of shares issued. The Dividend Per Share Ratio is calculated as follows:

$$\frac{\text{Total Dividend}}{\text{Number of Shares}}$$

Dividend Per Share Ratio is of special interest to the shareholders as the shareholders want to earn rewards on their investments in the form of dividends. The Dividend Per Share Ratio gives an indication as to the return per share that has been earned by the shareholders.

Dividend Cover Ratio:

The Dividend Cover Ratio compares the Net Profit available to Equity or Common Shareholders and compares it with the Dividends that are paid to the Equity or Common Shareholders. It is calculated as follows:

$$\frac{\text{Net Profit available to Equity or Common Shareholders (IACS)}}{\text{Dividends paid to Equity or Common Shareholders (Declared Dividend)}}$$

It can also be calculated as follows:

$$\frac{\text{Net Profit after Interest and Taxes}}{\text{Dividends paid to Equity or Common Shareholders (Declared Dividend)}}$$

The Dividend Cover Ratio gives an idea about the ease with which an organization can pay dividends to the shareholders. A high Dividend Cover Ratio indicates a good ability on part of the organization to pay dividends due to sufficient amount of retained profits whereas a low Dividend Cover Ratio indicates a low ability or difficulty on the part of the organization to pay dividends due to low level of retained profits.

Earnings Per Share (EPS):

Earnings Per Share (EPS) is the profit that each equity or common share is entitled to if dividend is declared to the equity or common shares that are outstanding in the books of accounts.

Earnings Per Share (EPS) calculation is done in two ways. One way is to calculate the Basic Earnings Per Share (EPS). The other way is to calculate Diluted Earnings Per Share (EPS). Basic Earnings Per Share (EPS) is the Earnings Per Share that is calculated for all equity or common shares that are outstanding at the end of a particular period. Diluted Earnings Per Share (EPS) is the Earnings Per Share (EPS) that is calculated for all potentially issuable and dilutive equity or common shares had been issued on the first day of a particular period.

Earnings Per Share (EPS) calculation is important because it is required for each public company to disclose Earnings Per Share (EPS) (both Basic Earnings Per Share (EPS) as well as Diluted Earnings Per Share (EPS)) in the financial statements.

Basic Earnings Per Share (BEPS):

Basic Earnings Per Share (BEPS) is calculated as follows:

Income Available to Common Shareholders (IAC)

Weighted-Average Number of Equity or Common Shares Outstanding (WANCSO)

Income Available to Common Shareholders (IAC) is calculated as follows:

Net Income
− Noncumulative Preference Shares dividends declared
− Cumulative Preference Shares dividends earned

The result of the calculation gives an indication as to the earnings that are available for distribution to the Common or Equity Shareholders.

Cumulative Preference Shares are shares that earn a certain percent of the par value of the share by way of dividend and this dividend does not have to be declared. It needs to be paid every year. If dividend on Cumulative Preference Shares has not been paid in a particular year, it needs to be paid first before any other dividend for Equity or Common Shares is declared. This means that the outstanding dividend on Cumulative Preference Shares has to be paid first along with the current year's dividend on Cumulative Preference Shares before Equity or Common Shares can earn dividend. In this respect, Cumulative Preference Shares are similar to bonds.

Non Cumulative Preference Shares are shares that are entitled to dividend only when dividend is declared by the company. So, when dividend on Preference Shares is declared, that money is no longer available to the Equity or Common Shareholders as it will hae to be paid to the Preference Shareholders.

If Preference Shares are not expressly stated to be cumulative, it is assumed that they are non cumulative.

Weighted-Average Number of Equity or Common Shares Outstanding (WANCSO) means the number of Equity or Common Shares equivalently outstanding for a particular period. For example, if 200 shares are purchased on July 1 of a particular year, the Weighted-Average Number of Equity or Common Shares Outstanding (WANCSO) will be 100 shares.

The weighting of the shares is done so as to ensure that a share that has not been outstanding or working for an entire year, it will not receive a full share in the profits. It can only have a claim to the profits to the extent that it has been outstanding.

In case a company reacquires its shares during the period for which the ratio is calculated, the shares are considered to be outstanding only till the time the company repurchased the shares i.e. till the time someone other than the company held the shares.

Shares issued during the year are included from the time of issuance till the time they are outstanding. For this purpose, it does not matter whether the shares are treasury shares or previously unissued shares as treasury shares are considered to be unissued till the time the company holds them. Shares are only considered to be outstanding if they are held by any person or entity other than the company.

Shares that are reacquired by the company are only considered to be outstanding till the date of reacquisition by the company.

In case of any stock dividends or stock splits, the stock dividends or stock splits are assumed to have happened at the beginning of the period under consideration. In case any stock dividends or stock splits occur after the period end but prior to the issuance of financial statements, the stock dividends or stock splits are treated as having occurred at the beginning of the first period in the financial statements.

Diluted Earnings Per Share (DEPS):

Diluted Earnings Per Share (DEPS) is based on the assumption that all equity or common shares that are potentially issuable and were outstanding at the end of the period have been issued i.e. exercised or converted at the beginning of the period. The potentially issuable shares could be in the form of options, warrant, convertible equity shares, convertible bonds that were outstanding at the end of the period. They are known as potentially issuable because they have not yet been issued and are not outstanding equity or common shares but they can be converted into equity or common shares through the act of someone other than the company.

This calculation assumes significance as any (potential) investor can understand the effect on Earnings Per Share (EPS) has these shares been issued and they were outstanding in the financial statements. This calculation assumes importance as if there are many such potentially issuable shares, the Earnings Per Share (EPS) would be greatly reduced had these shares been issued through the exercise of the option to convert the options, warrant, convertible equity shares, convertible bonds into equity or common shares.

However, it is important to note that the equity or common shares for thr options, warrant, convertible equity shares, convertible bonds should not have been issued for the period under consideration. If the equity or common shares have been issued, they will be taken into account for the calculation of Basic Earnings Per Share (BEPS).

Diluted Earnings Per Share (DEPS) is calculated as follows

1) Calculate Basic Earnings Per Share (BEPS)

2) Calculate the impact of options and warrants and add it to the Basic Earnings Per Share (BEPS)

3) Calculate the impact of convertible preference shares and convertible bonds on the Earnings Per Share (EPS)

4) Add dilutive convertible preference shares and dilutive convertible bonds and calculate the Intermediate Diluted Earnings Per Share (DEPS)

5) Calculate the final Diluted Earnings Per Share (DEPS)

Calculate Basic Earnings Per Share (BEPS):

Basic Earnings Per Share (BEPS) is calculated as follows:

Income Available to Common Shareholders (IAC)

Weighted-Average Number of Equity or Common Shares Outstanding (WANCSO)

Calculate the impact of options and warrants:

Unexpired (outstanding) options and warrants represent shares that are potentially issuable. Therefore, warrants and options are to be included in calculating Diluted Earnings Per Share (DEPS). The question arises as to the amount of impact of the options and warrants in the calculation of Diluted Earnings Per Share (DEPS).

For the calculation of the amount of shares to be added as impact of the unexpired options and warrants it has to be assumed that all the options were exercised at the beginning of the period. Although shares have not actually been issued, it is assumed that they are issued and it is also assumed that the company has received consideration in the form of cash as the exercise price of the option or warrant.

The company uses the money received as consideration for exercise of the warrants and options to repurchase its own shares at the average price for the year from the market. This has the effect of reducing the number of issued shares from the exercise of warrants or options. In case the exercise price of the options or warrants is greater than the average market price of the share there is no need for any calculation as the assumption then is that the warrants and options are not exercised. This is due to the fact that a rational person would rather buy shares at a lesser price in the open market rather than exercise options at a higher rate.

The company then nets together the shares that have been repurchased as well as the shares that have been issued due to the exercise of the options and warrants. This netting will yield the net number of shares issued due to the options or warrants. This net number of shares issued due to the options or warrants is added to the Weighted-Average Number of Equity or Common Shares Outstanding (WANCSO). This will yield the Intermediate Earnings Per Share

The entire calculation is hypothetical as no shares are actually repurchased or issued.

Calculate the impact of convertible preference shares and convertible bonds:

The effect of convertible preference shares and convertible bonds that were outstanding at the end of the prior period and the beginning of the period under consideration has to be taken into consideration. This is because they are hypothetically considered to have been issued at the beginning of the period under consideration and hence they would affect the Income Available to Common Shareholders (IAC) (by the determination of the more income that would be available to the shareholders) and the Weighted-Average Number of Equity or Common Shares Outstanding (WANCSO) (through the determination of conversion into equity shares of the and convertible preference shares and convertible bonds at the beginning of the period under consideration) would ultimately affect the Earnings Per Share (EPS).

Impact of Convertible Preference Shares:

The impact of Convertible Preference Shares on Earnings Per Share (EPS) is calculated as follows:

Dividends Earned (cumulative) or Declared (noncumulative)

Number of Common Shares into which the Preferred Shares are Converted

If shares had been issued from the preference shares through a specified conversion ratio at the beginning of the period, more equity or common shares would have been outstanding. Income available to equity or common shareholders would also increase because the dividend on preference shares would not have to be paid to the preference share holders by the company.

How much, if any, additional income would be available to the company would depend on the dividends declared or earned during the year as well as the type of preference shares that have been issued by the company.

In case the preference shares are cumulative in nature, the dividend that would have been payable on the cumulative preference shares would be saved and hence, would be available as additional income to the company and hence more income available to the equity or common shareholders.

In case the preference shares are non cumulative in nature the dividends declared during the year only (if any) would have been saved and hence, only the amount of dividends declared during the year would accrue as additional savings to the company and hence more income available to the equity or common shareholders .

The calculation needs to be done for each individual class of convertible preference shares.

Impact of Convertible Bonds:

The impact of Convertible Bonds on Earnings Per Share (EPS) is calculated as follows:

$$\frac{\text{Interest on the Bonds} \times (1 - \text{Tax Rate})}{\text{Number of Shares into which the Bonds are Converted}}$$

If shares had been issued from the bonds through a specified conversion ratio at the beginning of the period, more equity or common shares would have been outstanding. Income available to equity or common shareholders would also increase because the interest on bonds would not have to be paid to the bond holders by the company.

The interest on bonds would not have to be paid to the bond holders (saved interest), although an increase in income to the company, would not be wholly available to the equity or common shareholders as the taxable income of the company would increase. Interest paid is tax deductible. If bonds had been converted into equity or common shares, interest would not be paid and no tax deduction can be claimed hence taxable income is higher. Hence, the need to tax into consideration the tax effect by subtracting the effect of income taxes from the figure of saved interest (interest on bonds that would not have to be paid to the bond holders and hence an increase in income to the company).

The calculation needs to be done for each individual class of convertible bonds.

Add the impact of dilutive convertible preference shares and dilutive convertible bonds and calculate the Intermediate Diluted Earnings Per Share (DEPS):

The impact of dilutive convertible preference shares and dilutive convertible bonds on Earnings Per Share (EPS) needs to be added in a specific order. The preference share or bond that has the lowest effect on Earnings Per Share (EPS) is added back first for the calculation of Intermediate Diluted Earnings Per Share (IDPES). After addition of the preference share or bond that has the lowest effect on Earnings Per Share (EPS), the next preference share or bond that has the next lowest effect on Earnings Per Share (EPS) is added to the figure of Intermediate Diluted Earnings Per Share (IDPES). This process will continue until the Intermediate Diluted Earnings Per Share (IDPES) is lower than the next effect on Earnings Per Share (EPS).

Calculate the final Diluted Earnings Per Share (DEPS):

After the process of addition of preference share or bond that has the lowest effect on Earnings Per Share (EPS) to the Intermediate Diluted Earnings Per Share (IDPES) by a step by step process until the Intermediate Diluted Earnings Per Share (IDPES) is lower than the next effect on Earnings Per Share (EPS), the Intermediate Diluted Earnings Per Share (IDPES) is lower than the next effect on Earnings Per Share (EPS) then so calculated then becomes the final Diluted Earnings Per Share (DEPS).

Any preference shares or bonds that still remain after this process is done are disregarded as they are considered to be antidilutive as they would have the effect of increasing the Diluted Earnings Per Share (DEPS). Although these anti dilutive preference shares and bonds are not included in the calculation of the Diluted Earnings Per Share (DEPS), they need to be disclosed in the notes to the financial statements because there is a possibility that they may become dilutive in the future.

Earnings Per Share (EPS), whether Basic or Diluted is used as a measure of the success of an organization by the shareholders. Earnings Per Share (EPS) is used by the shareholders to determine share in profits available to them hence determining the overall profitability of an organization.

A high Earnings Per Share (EPS) is considered to be a sign of profitability that could lead to dividends or capital appreciation in the form of a rise in the price of shares. A high Earnings Per Share (EPS) over a period of time is a sign of a growing and prosperous organization with good and capable management.

On the other hand, a low Earnings Per Share (EPS) is considered negatively by shareholders as they do not expect dividends or capital appreciation in the form of rise in price of shares. A low Earnings Per Share (EPS) over a period of time is a sign of a stagnant and low growth organization. It could also imply weak management or bad policies that need to be reviewed.

Products and offerings may also need to be reviewed. An organization with a low Earnings Per Share (EPS) over time could imply a bad investment choice and even a credit risk.

REFERENCES:
1)http://pages.stern.nyu.edu/~%20adamodar/New_Home_Page/AccPrimer/inventory.htm
2)Irvin N. Gleim, Dale L. Flesher(2012) – Financial Planning, Performance and Control (Part 1), Gleim CMA Review, Sixteenth Edition.
3)Irvin N. Gleim, Dale L. Flesher(2012) – Financial Decision Making (Part 2), Gleim CMA Review, Sixteenth Edition.
4)Brian Hock, Lynn Roden, David Fairchild (2010) – Part 2 Financial Decision Making, Hock International.
5)Saurav Dutta, Tony Griffin, Karen L. Jett, Jan Kooiman, Lon Petro, Siaw-Peng Wan (2009) – CMA Learning System Part 2: Financial Decision Making, Version 3.0, Institute of Management Accountants (IMA).
6)Risk Management Association (2011) – Annual Statement Studies Financial Ratio Benchmarks 2011 2012 (www.rmahq.org).
7)Standards for the Calculation of Financial Ratios (2004)- The Danish Society of Financial Analysts, The Norwegian Society of Financial Analysts.
8)http://www.accountingcycle.org/Operating-Cycle.html
9)P Muralidhar (nd) – Ratio Analysis, Matrusri Institute of PG Studies, http://www.slideshare.net/Dharan178/ratio-analysis-2970642
10)http://www.qfinance.com/cash-flow-management-calculations/liquidity-ratio-analysis
11)http://www.allprojectreports.com/MBA-Projects/Finance-Project-Report/ratio-analysis/ratio-analysis-advantage-limitations-classification-financial-ratio-analysis.htm
12)http://www.demonstratingvalue.org/resources/financial-ratio-analysis
13)http://www3.nd.edu/~mgrecon/simulations/micromaticweb/financialratios.html
14)http://www.cliffsnotes.com/more-subjects/accounting/accounting-principles-ii/financial-statement-analysis/ratio-analysis
15)http://www.bized.co.uk/compfact/ratios/liquid1.htm
16)http://www.demonstratingvalue.org/resources/financial-ratio-analysis#Leverage
17)http://www.demonstratingvalue.org/resources/financial-ratio-analysis#Profitability
18)http://www.bized.co.uk/compfact/ratios/investor10.htm
19)http://en.wikibooks.org/wiki/AQA_Business_Studies/Ratio_Analysis
20)http://www.prenhall.com/divisions/bp/app/cfl/RA/MarketValueRatios.html
21)http://www.prenhall.com/divisions/bp/app/cfl/RA/DebtManagementRatios.html
22)http://www.investopedia.com/terms/s/shareholdersequity.asp
23)http://www.bized.co.uk/compfact/ratios/asset5.htm
24)Hemant R. Dani (2000) – Balance Sheets Content, Analysis and Interpretation, Vision Books Pvt Ltd.

DUPONT ANALYSIS

The analysis is known as Dupont Analysis because it was a company called Dupont that started using this method in the year 1919 as a means to analyze the effectiveness of the organization.

Different authors define the Dupont Analysis differently. Since Financial Analysis is subjective at times as the ratios are interpreted in context and different ratios have importance in different industries and sectors as well as in the estimate of analysts, these differences are natural. However, the effect is the linking together of some efficiency ratios with some profitability ratios.

It is calculated as follows:

Return on Assets * Return on Common Equity

The Dupont Analysis gives valuable insights to understanding the ratios. One use of the Dupont Analysis is to understand the relevance of the Return on Assets ratio to an organization. The Return on Assets can be analyzed as to its components and a better understanding of this ratio can be had including its component ratios. Links between the various ratios can be easily seen.

Return on Assets Ratio:

Return on Assets Ratio can be calculated as follows:

Net Income

Average Total Assets

Some formulae use year end balances instead of Average Balances.

The Return on Assets Ratio can be analyzed for its component ratios.

Asset Turnover Ratio:

The Asset Turnover Ratio is calculated as follows:

Net Sales

Average Total Assets

Some formulae use year end balances instead of Average Balances.

The Asset Turnover Ratio gives an idea about the efficient use of assets. The Asset Turnover Ratio helps understand how efficiently the assets are used to generate sales.

Profit Margin on Sales (Net Profit Margin Ratio):

The Profit Margin on Sales (Net Profit Margin Ratio) is calculated as follows:

$$\frac{\text{Net Income}}{\text{Net Sales}}$$

The Profit Margin on Sales (Net Profit Margin Ratio) helps understand how much of sales is converted into profits. The higher the ratio, the more efficiently the organization is run as this means that expenditures and costs are controlled. In case of an extremely low ratio, the indication is that costs and expenses need to be controlled. In case of an extremely high ratio, a possible indication is that the organization can expand and also look at other (new) business opportunities.

Return on Assets Ratio Breakup:

Return on Assets Ratio can therefore be calculated as follows:

Asset Turnover Ratio * Profit Margin on Sales (Net Profit Margin Ratio)

$$= \quad \frac{\text{Net Sales}}{\text{Average Total Assets}} \quad * \quad \frac{\text{Net Income}}{\text{Net Sales}}$$

Some formulae use year end balances instead of Average Balances.

Thus the Return on Assets ratio depends on the efficiency in the use of assets to generate sales as well as the efficiency in the control of costs and expenses and the ability to generate high sales and in turn, high profits. If one or both of these ratios changes, the Return on Assets ratio changes. Thus, if one or both of these ratios increases, the Return on Assets ratio increases. Similarly, one or both of these ratios decreases, the Return on Assets ratio is adversely affected.

Return on Equity (ROE):

Return on Equity (ROE) is the second component of Dupont Analysis. It is calculated as follows:

$$\frac{\text{Net Income}}{\text{Average Total Equity}}$$

Some formulae use year end balances instead of Average Balances.

The Return on Equity (ROE) Ratio gives an idea about the earnings that are earned by the organization for each amount of equity. The Return on Equity measures the efficiency with which the amount generated from shareholders (equity) is used. The Return on Equity Ratio can be used as a measure to understand the performance of the management of the organization.

The Return on Equity (ROE) ratio is made up of three ratios namely the Profit Margin on Sales (Net Income) Ratio, Asset Turnover Ratio and the Equity Multiplier. The Profit Margin on Sales (Net Income) Ratio, Asset Turnover Ratio are also part of the Return on Assets Ratio.

Equity Multiplier Ratio:

The Equity Multiplier Ratio is calculated as follows:

$$\frac{\text{Average Total Assets}}{\text{Average Total Equity}}$$

It can also be stated as follows:

$$\frac{1}{1 - \frac{\text{(Average Debt)}}{\text{(Average Assets)}}}$$

It can also be stated as follows:

$$1 + \frac{\text{(Average Debt)}}{\text{(Average Assets)}}$$

Some formulae use year end balances instead of Average Balances. When financial statements of multiple periods are available, average balances may be uses. In case information of a single period is available, year end balance may be used. This usually depends upon preference of the analyst.

The Equity Multiplier Ratio measures the leverage of the organization. The Equity Multiplier Ratio helps understand the assets that have been financed by the shareholders. In case money received from incurring debt is invested for the purposes of investments, growth and expansion, the remainder after repayment of interest and principal amount is retained by the shareholders. This return on equity is therefore leveraged.

Incurring debt means having to repay this debt through interest as well as principal payments. This is a fixed expense. Furthermore, in the event of liquidation of an organization, the creditors have preference over the shareholders for repayment of debt. It also means that there could be a deduction in tax liability as interest payments could be written off.

The smaller the proportion of the assets that have been financed by the shareholders, the larger is the Equity Multiplier. This means that the leverage is high. Similarly, the larger the proportion of the assets that have been financed by the shareholders, the smaller is the Equity Multiplier. This means that the leverage is low.

Asset Turnover Ratio:

The Asset Turnover Ratio is calculated as follows:

$$\frac{\text{Net Sales}}{\text{Average Total Assets}}$$

Some formulae use year end balances instead of Average Balances. When financial statements of multiple periods are available, average balances may be uses. In case information of a single period is available, year end balance may be used. This usually depends upon preference of the analyst.

The Asset Turnover Ratio gives an idea about the efficient use of assets. The Asset Turnover Ratio helps understand how efficiently the assets are used to generate sales.

Profit Margin on Sales (Net Profit Margin Ratio):

The Profit Margin on Sales (Net Profit Margin Ratio) is calculated as follows:

$$\frac{\text{Net Income}}{\text{Net Sales}}$$

The Profit Margin on Sales (Net Profit Margin Ratio) helps understand how much of sales is converted into profits. The higher the ratio, the more efficiently the organization is run as this means that expenditures and costs are controlled. In case of an extremely low ratio, the indication is that costs and expenses need to be controlled. In case of an extremely high ratio, a possible indication is that the organization can expand and also look at other (new) business opportunities.

Thus the Return on Equity Ratio can be calculated as follows:

Profit Margin on Sales (Net Profit Margin Ratio) * Asset Turnover Ratio * Equity Multiplier Ratio

$$= \quad \frac{\text{Net Income}}{\text{Net Sales}} \quad * \quad \frac{\text{Net Sales}}{\text{Average Total Assets}} \quad * \quad \frac{\text{Average Total Assets}}{\text{Average Total Equity}}$$

Some formulae use year end balances instead of Average Balances.

This means that Return on Equity (ROE) Ratio is affected by efficiency of operations as measured by the Profit Margin on Sales (Net Profit Margin Ratio) along with the efficiency with which the assets are used as measured by the Asset Turnover Ratio and the financial leverage of the organization as measured by the Equity Multiplier Ratio.

Change in any of these items will affect the Return on Equity (ROE) Ratio. Therefore, if any or all of these ratios show improvement, the Return on Equity Ratio will show improvement. Similarly, if any or all of these ratios show deterioration, the Return on Equity (ROE) Ratio will show a decline.

Thus, if the Profit Margin on Sales (Net Profit Margin Ratio) (the operations are run efficiently) shows improvement, this could mean that Asset Turnover Ratio (the assets could have been used more efficiently) could have improved. If the Equity Multiplier (leverage) is high, the Return on Equity (ROE) Ratio will also be high. Similarly, if the Return on Equity (ROE) Ratio shows a decline, the component ratios may be analyzed to understand the decline.

Return on Common Equity (ROCE) Ratio:

Return on Common or Ordinary Equity (ROCE) Ratio is calculated as follows:

$$\frac{\text{Net Income - Dividend on Preference Shares}}{\text{Average Common or Ordinary Equity}}$$

Some formulae use year end balances instead of Average Balances. When financial statements of multiple periods are available, average balances may be uses. In case information of a single period is available, year end balance may be used. This usually depends upon preference of the analyst.

Since preference dividend is paid to Preference Shareholders and not to Ordinary or Common Equity Shareholders, the dividend paid Preference Shareholders has to be subtracted from Net Income as this is income that will not be available to Ordinary or Common Equity Shareholders.

The Return on Common or Ordinary Equity (ROCE) Ratio is made up of three ratios namely The Profit Margin on Sales (Net Profit Margin Ratio), The Asset Turnover Ratio and The Equity Multiplier Ratio.

Profit Margin on Sales (Net Profit Margin Ratio):

The Profit Margin on Sales (Net Profit Margin Ratio) is calculated as follows:

$$\frac{\text{Net Income}}{\text{Net Sales}}$$

The Profit Margin on Sales (Net Profit Margin Ratio) helps understand how much of sales is converted into profits. The higher the ratio, the more efficiently the organization is run as this means that expenditures and costs are controlled. In case of an extremely low ratio, the indication is that costs and expenses need to be controlled. In case of an extremely high ratio, a possible indication is that the organization can expand and also look at other (new) business opportunities.

Asset Turnover Ratio:

The Asset Turnover Ratio is calculated as follows:

$$\frac{\text{Net Sales}}{\text{Average Total Assets}}$$

Some formulae use year end balances instead of Average Balances. When financial statements of multiple periods are available, average balances may be uses. In case information of a single period is available, year end balance may be used. This usually depends upon preference of the analyst.

The Asset Turnover Ratio gives an idea about the efficient use of assets. The Asset Turnover Ratio helps understand how efficiently the assets are used to generate sales.

Equity Multiplier Ratio:

The Equity Multiplier Ratio is calculated as follows:

$$\frac{\text{Average Total Assets}}{\text{Average Total Equity}}$$

Some formulae use year end balances instead of Average Balances. When financial statements of multiple periods are available, average balances may be uses. In case information of a single period is available, year end balance may be used. This usually depends upon preference of the analyst.

The Equity Multiplier Ratio measures the leverage of the organization. The Equity Multiplier Ratio helps understand the assets that have been financed by the shareholders. The smaller the proportion of the assets that have been financed by the shareholders, the larger is the Equity Multiplier. This means that the leverage is high. Similarly, the larger the proportion of the assets that have been financed by the shareholders, the smaller is the Equity Multiplier. This means that the leverage is low.

Thus the Return on Common or Ordinary Equity (ROCE) Ratio is calculated as follows:

Profit Margin on Sales (Net Profit Margin Ratio) * Asset Turnover Ratio * Equity Multiplier Ratio

$$= \frac{\text{Net Income}}{\text{Net Sales}} * \frac{\text{Net Sales}}{\text{Average Total Assets}} * \frac{\text{Average Total Assets}}{\text{Average Total Equity}}$$

Some formulae use year end balances instead of Average Balances. When financial statements of multiple periods are available, average balances may be uses. In case information of a single period is available, year end balance may be used. This usually depends upon preference of the analyst.

This means that Return on Common or Ordinary Equity (ROCE) Ratio is affected by efficiency of operations as measured by the Profit Margin on Sales (Net Profit Margin Ratio) along with the efficiency with which the assets are used as measured by the Asset Turnover Ratio and the financial leverage of the organization as measured by the Equity Multiplier Ratio.

Change in any of these items will affect the Return on Common or Ordinary Equity (ROCE) Ratio. Therefore, if any or all of these ratios show improvement, the Return on Common or Ordinary Equity (ROCE) Ratio will show improvement. Similarly, if any or all of these ratios show deterioration, the Return on Common or Ordinary Equity (ROCE) Ratio will show a decline.

Thus, if the Profit Margin on Sales (Net Profit Margin Ratio) (the operations are run efficiently) shows improvement, this could mean that Asset Turnover Ratio (the assets could have been used more efficiently) could have improved. If the Equity Multiplier (leverage) is high, the Return on Common or Ordinary Equity (ROCE) Ratio will also be high. Similarly, if the Return on

Common or Ordinary Equity (ROCE) Ratio shows a decline, the component ratios may be analyzed to understand the decline.

REFERENCES:

1)http://pages.stern.nyu.edu/~%20adamodar/New_Home_Page/AccPrimer/inventory.htm
2)Irvin N. Gleim, Dale L. Flesher(2012) – Financial Planning, Performance and Control (Part 1), Gleim CMA Review, Sixteenth Edition.
3)Irvin N. Gleim, Dale L. Flesher(2012) – Financial Decision Making (Part 2), Gleim CMA Review, Sixteenth Edition.
4)Brian Hock, Lynn Roden, David Fairchild (2010) – Part 2 Financial Decision Making, Hock International.
5)Saurav Dutta, Tony Griffin, Karen L. Jett, Jan Kooiman, Lon Petro, Siaw-Peng Wan (2009) – CMA Learning System Part 2: Financial Decision Making, Version 3.0, Institute of Management Accountants (IMA).
6)Risk Management Association (2011) – Annual Statement Studies Financial Ratio Benchmarks 2011 2012 (www.rmahq.org).
7)Standards for the Calculation of Financial Ratios (2004)- The Danish Society of Financial Analysts, The Norwegian Society of Financial Analysts.
8)http://www.accountingcycle.org/Operating-Cycle.html
9)P Muralidhar (nd) – Ratio Analysis, Matrusri Institute of PG Studies, http://www.slideshare.net/Dharan178/ratio-analysis-2970642
10)http://www.qfinance.com/cash-flow-management-calculations/liquidity-ratio-analysis
11)http://www.allprojectreports.com/MBA-Projects/Finance-Project-Report/ratio-analysis/ratio-analysis-advantage-limitations-classification-financial-ratio-analysis.htm
12)http://www.demonstratingvalue.org/resources/financial-ratio-analysis
13)http://www3.nd.edu/~mgrecon/simulations/micromaticweb/financialratios.html
14)http://www.cliffsnotes.com/more-subjects/accounting/accounting-principles-ii/financial-statement-analysis/ratio-analysis
15)http://www.bized.co.uk/compfact/ratios/liquid1.htm
16)http://www.demonstratingvalue.org/resources/financial-ratio-analysis#Leverage
17)http://www.demonstratingvalue.org/resources/financial-ratio-analysis#Profitability
18)http://www.bized.co.uk/compfact/ratios/investor10.htm
19)http://en.wikibooks.org/wiki/AQA_Business_Studies/Ratio_Analysis
20)http://www.prenhall.com/divisions/bp/app/cfl/RA/MarketValueRatios.html
21)http://www.prenhall.com/divisions/bp/app/cfl/RA/DebtManagementRatios.html
22)http://www.investopedia.com/terms/s/shareholdersequity.asp
23)http://www.bized.co.uk/compfact/ratios/asset5.htm
24)Hemant R. Dani (2000) – Balance Sheets Content, Analysis and Interpretation, Vision Books Pvt Ltd.

SUSTAINABLE EQUITY GROWTH RATE

The Sustainable Equity Growth Rate is the rate at which the organization can be expected to grow per year but without the need to increase the level of financing. The Net Income retained by the organization is indicative of growth to the common equity as the assumption is that this Net Income retained by the company will serve as finance to future growth and expansion and investment opportunities without the need to obtain finance externally.

The assessment of the Sustainable Equity Growth Rate is based on the assumption that dividend payout as well as Net Income retained by the company remain constant.

The Sustainable Equity Growth Rate is calculated as follows:

Return on Common Equity (ROCE) * (1-Dividend Payout Ratio)

Sustainable Equity Growth Rate assumes significance due to growing rate of failures of businesses. Some organizations fail because they fail to earn enough revenue to cover costs and incur losses that cannot be sustained. Other fail because they take contracts that they cannot fulfill keeping in view their obligations, assets as well as size. Some others fail because they attempt to grow at a faster rate than can be maintained.

Sustainable Equity Growth Rate will therefore help understand the rate at which an organization can grow without having the need to have external sources of finance. Sustainable Equity Growth can be achieved when there is a balance between the Dividend Payout Ratio and the retention of earnings in order to reinvest into operations for growth and investment.

As the Sustainable Equity Growth Rate increases, there is an increased ability to take on additional debt on favorable terms without the risk of default or insolvency. In case an organization is growing at a rate that is greater than the Sustainable Equity Growth Rate, the need for external sources of financing would arise.

If the Dividend Payout Ratio is high, less money is retained for growth, expansion and investment. Hence the need for external financing would be high. In such a scenario, the Leverage and the Total Debt Ratios assume significance. In case these ratios are low, external financing could be obtained on favorable terms. However if these ratios are high, there is a risk of having unfavorable credit terms as well as default and even insolvency over a period of time.

Return on Common Equity (ROCE) Ratio:

Return on Common Equity (ROCE) Ratio is calculated as follows:

$$\text{Net Income - Dividend on Preference Shares}$$

$$\text{Average Common Equity}$$

Some formulae use year end balances instead of Average Balances. When financial statements of multiple periods are available, average balances may be uses. In case information of a single period is available, year end balance may be used. This usually depends upon preference of the analyst.

Dividend Payout Ratio:

Dividend Payout Ratio is calculated as follows:

$$\text{Dividends to Common Or Equity Shareholders}$$

$$\text{Income Available to Common or Equity Shareholders (IACS)}$$

This ratio gives an idea as to the amount of earnings or Net Income that is distributed to the shareholders as dividend and hence not retained by the company for growth, expansion or investment activities.

Usually in the early years of an organization, the Dividend Payout Ratio is low as there are losses and expenses related to incorporation have to be written off and when profits are declared, they are retained by the organization for growth, expansion or investment activities.

Income Available to Common (Equity) Shareholders (IACS):

Income Available to Common (Equity) Shareholders (IACS) is calculated as follows:

> Net Income
> − Noncumulative preferred dividends declared
> − Cumulative preferred dividends earned

REFERENCES:

1)http://pages.stern.nyu.edu/~%20adamodar/New_Home_Page/AccPrimer/inventory.htm
2)Irvin N. Gleim, Dale L. Flesher(2012) – Financial Planning, Performance and Control (Part 1), Gleim CMA Review, Sixteenth Edition.
3)Irvin N. Gleim, Dale L. Flesher(2012) – Financial Decision Making (Part 2), Gleim CMA Review, Sixteenth Edition.
4)Brian Hock, Lynn Roden, David Fairchild (2010) – Part 2 Financial Decision Making, Hock International.

5)Saurav Dutta, Tony Griffin, Karen L. Jett, Jan Kooiman, Lon Petro, Siaw-Peng Wan (2009) – CMA Learning System Part 2: Financial Decision Making, Version 3.0, Institute of Management Accountants (IMA).

6)Risk Management Association (2011) – Annual Statement Studies Financial Ratio Benchmarks 2011 2012 (www.rmahq.org).

7)Standards for the Calculation of Financial Ratios (2004)- The Danish Society of Financial Analysts, The Norwegian Society of Financial Analysts.

8)http://www.accountingcycle.org/Operating-Cycle.html

9)P Muralidhar (nd) – Ratio Analysis, Matrusri Institute of PG Studies, http://www.slideshare.net/Dharan178/ratio-analysis-2970642

10)http://www.qfinance.com/cash-flow-management-calculations/liquidity-ratio-analysis

11)http://www.allprojectreports.com/MBA-Projects/Finance-Project-Report/ratio-analysis/ratio-analysis-advantage-limitations-classification-financial-ratio-analysis.htm

12)http://www.demonstratingvalue.org/resources/financial-ratio-analysis

13)http://www3.nd.edu/~mgrecon/simulations/micromaticweb/financialratios.html

14)http://www.cliffsnotes.com/more-subjects/accounting/accounting-principles-ii/financial-statement-analysis/ratio-analysis

15)http://www.bized.co.uk/compfact/ratios/liquid1.htm

16)http://www.demonstratingvalue.org/resources/financial-ratio-analysis#Leverage

17)http://www.demonstratingvalue.org/resources/financial-ratio-analysis#Profitability

18)http://www.bized.co.uk/compfact/ratios/investor10.htm

19)http://en.wikibooks.org/wiki/AQA_Business_Studies/Ratio_Analysis

20)http://www.prenhall.com/divisions/bp/app/cfl/RA/MarketValueRatios.html

21)http://www.prenhall.com/divisions/bp/app/cfl/RA/DebtManagementRatios.html

22)http://www.investopedia.com/terms/s/shareholdersequity.asp

23)http://www.bized.co.uk/compfact/ratios/asset5.htm

24)Hemant R. Dani (2000) – Balance Sheets Content, Analysis and Interpretation, Vision Books Pvt Ltd.

DIFFERENCES IN DEFINITIONS

Reasons For Difference In Definitions Of Return Of Assets (ROA) AND Return On Equity (ROE):

The concept of Return, Assets and Equity are defined differently by different people. Some analysts prefer to use the term Return on Invested Capital rather than using terms like Return on Equity or Return on Assets.

Thus the definition of Return, Assets and Equity is usually left in the hands of the management of the organization. How the management will define these terms will depend on the intent of the management as to why and what calculation is being done.

How to define the term Equity in the Return on Invested Capital (ROIC) Ratio:

The term equity broadly includes Preference Shares as well as Equity or Common Shares. For the calculation of the Return on Equity (ROE) ratio, Equity can include both Preference Shares as well as Equity or Common Shares. However for the purpose of calculating Return on Common Equity (ROCE) ratio, only Equity or Common Shares are used.

In case Preference Shares are included in the calculation, it has to be determined whether they are cumulative or non cumulative in nature. In case the Preference Shares are cumulative, the cumulative dividend earned for the period is to be subtracted from the Net Income (NI) whether the dividend has been declared or not. In case the Preference Shares are not cumulative in nature, the dividend declared for the period is to be subtracted from the figure of Net Income (NI).

How to define the term Assets in the Return on Invested Capital (ROIC) Ratio:

Total Assets are defined differently. Assets can be defined only as Operating Assets to the exclusion of Intangible Assets, Investment Securities and other assets.

Assets can also be defined to the exclusion or elimination of depreciation. Assets can also be calculated to exclude Idle or Unproductive assets.

Assets can also be defined as Net Assets where Assets can be calculated as Net Assets less Net Liabilities. This would stress the role of Long Term Capital.

Assets can be defined to include Equity or Common Share Capital and exclude Preferred Stock and Shares. This would focus on the return generated for the Ordinary or Equity Shareholders.

Assets can also be defined to include Equity or Ordinary Share Capital and the Long Term Debt. This would include the long term capitalization and emphasize on the sources of long term financing which includes the shareholders as well as the long term creditors.

Assets can also be defined as the Invested Capital that includes both Equity or Ordinary Share Capital as well as Debt.

Assets can also be valued at Market Value rather than the Book Value. However, the value of Intangible

Assets can be measured at their Book Value rather than Market Value as financial statements are not supposed to measure the Intangible Assets at Market Value.

Some people will merely look at the Assets side of the Balance Sheet to define assets. Some others will define Total Assets as the sum total of Total Liabilities and Total Equity. If this definition is used in the calculation of Return on Assets (ROA) ratio, it gives an idea about the return to the organization from the use of its assets.

When this definition is used in the calculation of the Return on Invested Capital (ROIC) Ratio, distinction between the sources of financing is not made as the emphasis is only on the operating performance.

How to define the term Return in the Return on Invested Capital (ROIC) Ratio:

The figure of Return that is used in the Return on Invested Capital (ROIC) Ratio will depend on how the term Invested Capital is defined.

If the term Invested Capital is defined to mean Total Long Term Debt and Total Equity or Total Assets, the Return would be defined as Income Before Interest Expense as Interest Expense is payment made for the receipt of debt capital. The payment made to the suppliers of Equity Capital (dividends) are also to be disregarded.

If the term Invested Capital is defined to mean Ordinary or Common Equity Share Capital, the Return is to be defined as the Income Available to Common or Equity Shareholders (IACS). In order to calculate Income Available to Common or Equity Shareholders (IACS) the dividends on Preference Shares needs to be subtracted from the figure of Net Income (NI). In case of Cumulative Preference Shares, the dividends need to be subtracted irrespective of whether dividends have been declared or not. In case of Non Cumulative Preference Shares, the dividends need to be subtracted when they are earned. This is due to the fact that Preference Shares have a priority in payment of dividend over the Equity Shareholders.

When the company is a holding company and has the income and assets and liabilities of the subsidiary or subsidiaries consolidated in its financial statements then the definition of the word Return will change accordingly.

When a subsidiary is partially owned and the interest in the subsidiary is a non controlling interest, the income of such a subsidiary must be deducted from the figure of Net Income (NI) in the financial statements. However, all of the subsidiary's assets will be included in the Consolidated Balance Sheet.

If the term Invested Capital is defined to mean Total Assets the figure of Income would include the Income or Loss of the company inclusive of the non controlling owner.

If the term Invested Capital is defined to mean Equity Capital, if the interest in the non controlled subsidiary is excluded, the Income or loss from such a subsidiary is also to be excluded.

As a rule, no matter how the term Invested Capital is defined, Income Taxes have to be subtracted from the figure of Return or Net Income (NI). This is due to the fact that Income Taxes reduce the Net Income (NI) available to the company.

REFERENCES:
1)http://pages.stern.nyu.edu/~%20adamodar/New_Home_Page/AccPrimer/inventory.htm
2)Irvin N. Gleim, Dale L. Flesher(2012) – Financial Planning, Performance and Control (Part 1), Gleim CMA Review, Sixteenth Edition.
3)Irvin N. Gleim, Dale L. Flesher(2012) – Financial Decision Making (Part 2), Gleim CMA Review, Sixteenth Edition.
4)Brian Hock, Lynn Roden, David Fairchild (2010) – Part 2 Financial Decision Making, Hock International.
5)Saurav Dutta, Tony Griffin, Karen L. Jett, Jan Kooiman, Lon Petro, Siaw-Peng Wan (2009) – CMA Learning System Part 2: Financial Decision Making, Version 3.0, Institute of Management Accountants (IMA).
6)Risk Management Association (2011) – Annual Statement Studies Financial Ratio Benchmarks 2011 2012 (www.rmahq.org).
7)Standards for the Calculation of Financial Ratios (2004)- The Danish Society of Financial Analysts, The Norwegian Society of Financial Analysts.
8)http://www.accountingcycle.org/Operating-Cycle.html
9)P Muralidhar (nd) – Ratio Analysis, Matrusri Institute of PG Studies, http://www.slideshare.net/Dharan178/ratio-analysis-2970642
10)http://www.qfinance.com/cash-flow-management-calculations/liquidity-ratio-analysis
11)http://www.allprojectreports.com/MBA-Projects/Finance-Project-Report/ratio-analysis/ratio-analysis-advantage-limitations-classification-financial-ratio-analysis.htm
12)http://www.demonstratingvalue.org/resources/financial-ratio-analysis
13)http://www3.nd.edu/~mgrecon/simulations/micromaticweb/financialratios.html
14)http://www.cliffsnotes.com/more-subjects/accounting/accounting-principles-ii/financial-statement-analysis/ratio-analysis
15)http://www.bized.co.uk/compfact/ratios/liquid1.htm
16)http://www.demonstratingvalue.org/resources/financial-ratio-analysis#Leverage
17)http://www.demonstratingvalue.org/resources/financial-ratio-analysis#Profitability
18)http://www.bized.co.uk/compfact/ratios/investor10.htm
19)http://en.wikibooks.org/wiki/AQA_Business_Studies/Ratio_Analysis
20)http://www.prenhall.com/divisions/bp/app/cfl/RA/MarketValueRatios.html

21)http://www.prenhall.com/divisions/bp/app/cfl/RA/DebtManagementRatios.html
22)http://www.investopedia.com/terms/s/shareholdersequity.asp
23)http://www.bized.co.uk/compfact/ratios/asset5.htm
24)Hemant R. Dani (2000) – Balance Sheets Content, Analysis and Interpretation, Vision Books Pvt Ltd.

HOW IS RATIO ANALYSIS USED

Ratio Analysis is used by different types of investors. Each of them will have a different use for Ratio Analysis. The use of Ratio Analysis would depend on the situation in which it is used. However it is used, the key is to diversify the portfolio as well as to reduce the risk of the entire portfolio as well as the risk of loss in an individual investment.

One of the uses of Ratio Analysis is to decide on an investment strategy. Based on the results of the analysis, the investor or the analyst would decide whether to invest in a particular security. The main reason for the use of Ratio Analysis in this situation is to make sure that the company that is being invested in has strong fundamentals. Needless to say, when investment has already been made in the company, Ratio Analysis helps to determine whether to hold or sell.

Ratio Analysis is also used to determine the value of a company. The financial health of a company can be determined by the Price – Earnings Ratio, Price – Sales Ratio, Debt to Equity Ratio etc. Ratio Analysis is also used in situations of Mergers and Acquisitions in order to determine the value of the company in order to make an offer of takeover as well as for the valuation of the Goodwill of the company.

Ratio Analysis gives an idea about the Earnings of the Company. The Earnings of the company are extremely important to investors. This figure gives an idea not only about the financial situation of the company but also as to dividends.

Earnings are used by investors to forecast dividends. It is also used to forecast capital appreciation as well as growth of the company. Low or negative earnings do not always mean that the company is a bad investment prospect. Younger companies often have negative earnings and they grow as they age and growth can be rapid.

Earnings can also be used by the management of the organization to determine profitability as well as productivity of the organization. This can help in comparison with the past trends, comparison with competitors and benchmarks as well as indication for the future as well as room for improvement.

Ratio Analysis also helps understand the relationship between assets and liabilities, giving an idea about the solvency of the organization as well as the need to borrow and working capital needs.

Ratio Analysis helps understand trends over time and thus help in budgeting, planning as well as chart the strategy for future growth as need for borrowing and expansion.

Along with Earnings, the EPS (Earnings per Share) is very often used by investors in order to determine growth, capital appreciation as well as dividend prospects. The main reason for the use of EPS (Earnings per Share) is that while Earnings gives an overall figure, EPS (Earnings per

Share) gives the figure per share. It thus takes into account the Earnings as well as the number of shares outstanding.

Another ratio that is consistently used is the Price Earnings Ratio. This ratio is used to find out whether the company is overvalued or undervalued. In case the Market Price is higher as compared to the Earnings, the company is overvalued. The opposite is also true. The Price Earnings Ratio helps determine whether the investor would invest in the stock or would hold or sell the stock.

Ratio Analysis is also used by Value Investors in order to determine whether a company is overvalued or undervalued in the stock market. Such investors buy undervalued companies and wait for the price to rise in order to sell and earn a profit. The exact opposite strategy is used in the case of an overvalued company. They sell the shares of an overvalued company at an appropriate time and avoid losses when prices go down.

Ratio Analysis is used to determine the strengths and weakness of an organization from a financial point of view. Financial statements give an idea about the profitability, solvency, liquidity, activity of an organization as well as the efficiency in use of assets which gives an idea about managerial ability giving a good measure of the operational efficiency of the organization. This will help determine whether the organization is worth investing in. An organization that is going to grow and expand in the future is a good investment whereas organizations that do not show strong financial statements may not be worth investing in.

Weaknesses if any in the organizational performance can be taken note of by the management and remedial measures can be instituted by the management in order to better performance in the future. Strengths of an organization can be converted into competitive advantage and can be strengthened further.

Ratio Analysis helps understand individual items in the financial statements as they are used in the ratios so as to make comparisons easier. For example, if an organization wants to look at the increase or decrease in Administrative costs, it can only look at the Profit and Loss Account (Statement of Income and Loss) and analyze the individual items making up the Administrative costs and establish a trend for a number of periods.

Ratio Analysis can be used to determine the future financial position of an organization based on the current financial statements. Past ratios develop a trend over time that can help forecast the future financial performance of an organization provided certain economic conditions remain similar in the future. Thus, business cycles can be established and can help the organization take better financial as well as operational decisions.

Ratio Analysis is not used to determine market behavior or the overall state of the market. Ratio Analysis focuses only on the financials of the company in order to determine whether to buy, hold or sell a security.

Ratio Analysis is also used to determine whether there is evidence of window dressing. This is when management tries to cook the books. When ratios do not make any sense and do not follow any pattern, there are certain indications that management of the company is not being entirely honest with the books of accounts.

Ratio Analysis is also used to determine how the company is doing vis – a – vis the competitors. Ratio Analysis can also be used to compare the performance of different departments within an organization as well as that of different branches and different subsidiaries of an organization. The ratios of a company can be compared to its nearest competitors in the industry in order to determine the strength of the company. The ratios of the company can also be compared against the average ratios in the industry as well as the sector in which it operates in order to determine the health and growth prospects of the company.

Various stakeholders can also use Ratio Analysis to take decisions. Creditors can determine the credit worthiness of an organization and determine terms of credit; suppliers can determine whether to do or continue to do business with the organization as well as to determine the terms with which to do business with the organization. Shareholders can analyze the profitability of the organization and determine whether dividend can be earned or not as well as whether to hold the shares or sell and thus make investment decisions.

Not only ratios but certain qualitative factors can be studied that help determine the company's prospects as a viable investment. Brand Recognition, Patents, Proprietary Technology, Key Executives as well as Board Members help determine the direction in which the company is heading as well as potential for future earnings and growth.

However, the best use of Ratio Analysis is made when it is used in combination with the other methods of analyzing a company. More often than not, Ratio Analysis is used along with Technical Analysis. Even when an in depth analysis is done. There is no guarantee of success in a hundred percent of investments made. There will be some successes while some other investment strategies may not work out as well as the market is unpredictable. Economists of the stature of Burton Malkiel have suggested that neither Ratio Analysis nor technical analysis would prove useful in outperforming the markets. The markets cannot be outperformed. This is the basic rule of the markets.

However, care has to be taken while using this method of analysis. Ratio Analysis cannot be used for speculation. Ratio Analysis does not help in case of speculation or intraday trading. This method of analysis helps find the true value of the company and is therefore useful to those interested in a medium to long term investment strategy. Anyone who indulges in speculation or intraday trading does not prefer Ratio Analysis as this method requires some time to analyze a stock and the movements in the stock market on a day to day basis are somewhat volatile. Such investors usually prefer Technical Analysis. Ratio Analysis is of great help to anyone who is willing to ignore short term volatility in the market and opt for consistent return in the form of dividends and capital appreciation over the medium term and the long term.

REFERENCES:

1)http://www.investopedia.com/exam-guide/cfa-level-1/financial-ratios/uses-limitations-ratios.asp
2)http://www.cliffsnotes.com/more-subjects/accounting/accounting-principles-ii/financial-statement-analysis/need-for-financial-statement-analysis
3)http://my.safaribooksonline.com/book/accounting/9788131774960/chapter-3dot-accounting-ratios-for-financial-statement-analysis/ch3_sub3_7_xhtml
4)http://accountingexplained.com/financial/ratios/advantages-limitations
5)http://www.wisegeek.com/what-are-the-uses-of-ratio-analysis.htm
6)http://www.list4everything.com/uses-of-ratio-analysis.html
7)http://accountlearning.blogspot.in/2010/02/importance-and-advantages-of-ratio.html
8)http://www.readyratios.com/reference/analysis/ratio_analysis.html

ADVANTAGES AND DISADVANTAGES OF FUNDAMENTAL ANALYSIS

Ratio Analysis is based on analyzing the economic factors and arriving at a conclusion as to an investment decision. Economic, political, social forces that determine the supply and demand are analyzed and future prospects of a stock are analyzed. Like any method or system, Ratio Analysis also has its advantages and disadvantages.

ADVANTAGES:

Ratio Analysis helps arrive at the value of an organization. Buy or sell decisions can be made based on the worth of the company at a particular days' price. If the value of a share is greater than the price at which it is traded, it is a good buy as the share is undervalued and the price would likely increase in the future whereas if the value of a share is lesser than the price at which it is traded, it is overvalued and hence the decision to not buy the share or to sell it would be wise as the price may decrease in the future.

Ratio Analysis takes a long term view and hence helps analyze the multi year as well as multi decade trends and helps take advantage of them by investing in stocks that will increase in price over a medium to long term. It can therefore be said that Ratio Analysis has an approach to trading that is more realistic.

Ratio Analysis can help analyze the creditworthiness of an organization. Based on the financial statements, various ratios can be calculated that will help determine whether the company is worthy of extending credit or not.

The management of an organization can also be evaluated based on the financial statements and the various profitability and efficiency ratios that can be calculated based on these financial statements.

It can therefore be said that the pulse of the company can be understood through Ratio Analysis. The financials help understand whether the company's financial position is in a good state or not. It is also possible to spot a good investment before the market. For example, a company that is in a sector or an industry that is expected to make good progress can be spotted as a good investment if the share of the company is underpriced and the financials of the company are sound.

Observing and learning fundamentals of different industries, sectors of the economy as well as different markets and economies will lead to a greater understanding and knowledge of the global markets. Through the use of Ratio Analysis, prediction of economic conditions becomes possible and easy. The picture of the general economic health becomes clear and awareness of the happenings in the economy is achieved.

Ratio Analysis helps understand the business as well as business models. Therefore, it provides a strong basis for understanding the value of a company. The Fundamental Analyst invests in a stock that has strong business model and has a high margin of safety with indicators that provide the strong possibility of good performance or possibility for high growth and thus provides a growth in wealth in terms of dividend and capital appreciation.

The performance of an organization could be affected by various small factors that could go together. An analysis of the financial statements of an organization will help understand these factors and will help in getting a better understanding of the functioning of the organization as well as the effect of the industry as well as the overall economy on the organization as well as the overall state of the industry and the economy.

Ratio Analysis can be used in Forensic Accounting. The trends of the various ratios over a period of time can be compared and comparison can also be made with the average trend in the industry over time and significant variations can be compared and analyzed for possibility of fraud in the organization.

Even if fraud does not exist, the variations can be analyzed for possible improvement areas. Positive variances could indicate significant strengths in an organization that could be developed into special abilities for the organization that could lead to increase in revenue and profits as well as greater efficiency in operations.

Ratio Analysis is based on the concept that one thing leads to another. Ratio Analysis believes that performance in the past will give a fair indication as to future performance which means that past performance leads to or gives an indication of future performance. Ratio Analysis attempts to identify the factors that will lead to performance in the future. Ratio Analysis is thus intuitively appealing.

Ratio Analysis is based on the premise that there is a relationship between the accounting factors that are analyzed with each other. When accounts are compared with each other, a better idea is got about the inter relationship of the various factors that affect the accounts as well as the factors that affect the performance of an organization, an industry as well as the economy as a whole.

Ratio Analysis is based on mathematical analysis of data such as use of ratios and comparison with industry and sector ratios. Personal bias or prediction does not enter the picture. Analysts and traders prefer to rely on objective data in order to make a judgment rather than rely on personal bias and prediction. Hence the accuracy of Ratio Analysis in locating a profitable investment is greater.

Due to the preference for objective judgment, Ratio Analysis has developed and improved the techniques used to analyze stocks. An example of a well developed technique would be Chaos Theory that is used in futures analysis that is used by futures traders.

DISADVANTAGES:

One of the disadvantages of Ratio Analysis is the amount of data that needs to be analyzed. Different political, social, economic indicators etc need to be analyzed in order to make a decision. Moreover, different stocks from different industries mean that different industries need to be analyzed separately. Different analysts give importance to different ratios. The ordinary investor could be baffled as to which analyst or which ratios to rely on while making an investment decision.

Data required for Ratio Analysis may not be available easily and even if it is available, it may not be free. Even if data is available, in order to make a prediction as to price, a relationship between the different variables (items in the Balance Sheet and Profit and Loss Account as well as between the ratios) needs to be established as many variables are interlinked and hence affect each other. To establish such a relationship may be difficult if not impossible.

Ratio Analysis involves calculation of a number of ratios. No single ratio can give an idea about the organization or industry that is being analyzed. Moreover, the calculation of the ratios is not sufficient. The ratios have to be analyzed taking into consideration a number of factors such as the state of the economy, the competitor ratios, the industry in which the organization operates etc. Variances of the ratios with expectations as well as with industry trends also need to be analyzed.

Financial statements include items that are of an extraordinary nature or even non operating items. The effect of these items needs to be understood and a decision has to be made to either include or exclude these items from analysis that will help form a judgment. Items that are not in the ordinary course of business are better excluded from analysis as they are not everyday occurrences and may not recur in the future. The entire process is very time consuming as well as complicated at times.

In Ratio Analysis, financial data of either the previous quarter or the previous year is analyzed. Hence, there is a delay in terms of time i.e. from the time the financials are released till the analysis is done. In this time, the market dynamics may have changed. The impact of various factors such as changed interest rates may not be understood till the publication of the financials of the next quarter or the next year. Fundamentals of a company may change from the time the financials are analyzed till investment is made. From the time investment is made till either dividend is declared or capital appreciation occurs, the fundamentals may change and may lead to loss.

Ratio Analysis is based on the premise that there is a relationship between the accounting factors that are analyzed with each other. Therefore, the validity of any ratio will also depend on the accounts that are being compared. In case the accounts being compared with each other are not related, an ill formed opinion may be formed.

There are a lot of macro and micro indicators that need to be analyzed in order to come to a conclusion. This is not only time consuming and labor intensive, it can also be convincing to a novice investor or a beginner who may struggle to grasp the various concepts and the intricacies of analysis.

Ratio Analysis is based on the prediction of future results through projecting from past information. This principle is known as extrapolation. The drawback is to examine whether the numbers that are extrapolated are realistic or not. An example may be that the trend for a particular stock may be up but the market may be saturated. In such a case, rather than the trend going up, it may actually flatten. Extrapolation may not always give positive results and there are times when a wrong decision may be made.

Ratio Analysis tends to be labor intensive. It requires a lot of human labor and considerable time Not everybody understands the different ratios as well as the in depth analysis that is needed to conduct Ratio Analysis. Ratio Analysis is usually conducted by organizations that employ a team in order to make investment decisions as well as by individuals who are trained in such matters. The ordinary public will find it difficult to conduct Ratio Analysis.

So many different ratios need to be analyzed that it is tedious and time consuming to conduct Ratio Analysis. There are some analysts who use particular ratios such as P/E (Price Earnings) Ratio, EPS (Earnings Per Share), Dividend Yield etc but the data needs to be searched for in the financial results of the company and financial results of a few quarters and a few years at least need to be considered to establish a trend and make a judgment about a particular stock.

Data such as the Balance Sheet and Profit and Loss Account may be easily doctored. Creative Accounting and Window Dressing can be used to make the financial performance seem better than it actually is. Reliance on such data to make an investment decision can lead to faulty analysis and investment decisions leading to losses. The accounting scandals such as Enron are a case in point where creative accounting was used to make financial results look better than they actually were, leading investors to question the validity of financial statements.

Different accounting methods give different results. Financial accounting methods such as stock valuation, inventory valuation, depreciation etc can be valued differently. Ratio calculation will differ based on the valuation methods used. Management can value these items in such a way that ratios calculated will yield positive figures. Some analysts will either revalue these ratios at a lower value or will not include these ratios in making an investment decision.

The performance of an organization could be affected by various small factors that could go together. Focusing on a single large factor can lead to misunderstanding of the performance of the organization.

Many items in the financial statements are stated in the financial statements based on the Historical Cost approach. Historical cost approach may not reflect the true picture as the Fair

Value and the Market Value may differ from the Historical Cost. Ratios that are calculated based on these Historical Costs may not give a true picture of the performance of an organization as well as the state of affairs in the organization.

The analysis of large conglomerates becomes difficult as their performance may not be able to be compared with smaller organizations and an equivalent competitor may not be found at all times for comparison leading to an incomplete analysis of such organizations.

Ratio Analysis will not give an exact idea at what price exactly the stock should be purchased or sold. It will only give an indication as to whether the stock should be invested in, held or sold. The price at which the stock should be bought or sold can be better understood by Technical Analysis.

Financial statements consist of simplified items as well as summaries that classify the economic events in order to present information that can be analyzed and understood by all stakeholders. In some cases, these simplified items and summaries can be relevant and recoverable whereas as at other times, they may not be recoverable.

Financial statements consist of items that are affected by inflation and other economic factors. If these factors are not taken into consideration while analyzing the financial statements and calculation of financial ratios, the comparison of ratios over a period of time will lead to distorted results and will not give a true picture of the financial position of the organization or industry that is being analyzed.

As the share price is based on market sentiment, there are times the market is extremely bearish or extremely bullish. Due to these phenomenons, the stock price can swing from extremely undervalued to extremely overvalued. When the share is overpriced, Ratio Analysis will lead to the investor exiting too early or staying out of the market entirely and hence the investor may miss out on huge profits.

There are times when Ratio Analysis could give conflicting results. The organization analyzed may be doing well but the industry results may not be good. Similarly, the organization may do worse than the industry average. Different ratios in the same company may yield conflicting results.

In periods of relative economic stability, Ratio Analysis can prove to be very effective however in volatile economies where economies experience great uncertainty and in periods of high inflationary tendencies, Ratio Analysis over a period time, to compare financial statements over a period of time would be difficult and at times even unhelpful.

Different analysts may arrive at different conclusions based on their understanding, experience, knowledge, expectations etc. as the interpretation of Ratio Analysis is subjective. It is quite possible that different analysts may give conflicting advice on the same stock. One example of the difference in conclusions of Fundamental Analysts may be in the calculation of Fair Value. Analysts may arrive at different conclusions regarding Fair Value regarding a company. Moreover, since different industries and markets have different norms regarding valuation, the opinion of analysts may differ significantly. While taking into consideration the financial fundamentals, the reaction to the stock in the market may be ignored.

For investors interested in short term results, Ratio Analysis may prove frustrating. Ratio Analysis may help find a company to invest that has strong fundamentals and financials. However, the share price of a company may not move immediately. It may take some time to move. At times, it could even take months or years to move as share prices are based on the sentiment in the market. A good company may be unnoticed by investors and the market even for a long time. If the company has a good dividend policy, the shareholder will earn a good return on investment but will have to wait for capital appreciation.

Ratio Analysis involves only numerical analysis of an organization's performance. Qualitative factors such as customer loyalty, the reputation of an organization in the market, corporate social responsibility initiatives taken by the organization, employee morale, research and development towards making new products etc are ignored in Ratio Analysis.

REFERENCES:

1) http://stockmarketmangalindak.blogspot.in/2012/03/what-are-advantages-and-disadvantages.html
2) http://rainydaytrader.com/FundamentalAnalysis.html
3) http://elliottanalysis.com/2013/07/28/the-advantages-and-disadvantages-of-fundamental-analysis/
4) http://www.thewizardtrader.com/Education/FundamentalAnalysis.aspx
5) http://www.euroinvestor.com/ei-news/2012/02/12/stock-school-5-important-elements-in-fundamental-analysis/15694
6) http://wallstreetfool.com/2013/07/24/fundamental-analysis-vs-technical-analysis/
7) http://www.pcbbb.com/advantages-and-disadvantages--disadvantages-of-fundamental-analysis-1157.html
8) http://www.extraordinaryinvestor.com/fundamental-analysis-benefits.html
9) S&P Composite real price-earnings ratio image: By SP500pe.svg: Zane Selvans derivative work: AJabberWok (SP500pe.svg) [CC-BY-SA-3.0-2.5-2.0-1.0 (www.creativecommons.org/licenses/by-sa/3.0) or GFDL (www.gnu.org/copyleft/fdl.html)], via Wikimedia Commons
10) http://www.princeton.edu/~achaney/tmve/wiki100k/docs/Fundamental_analysis.html
11) http://www.forexfraud.com/learn-forex-trading/fundamental-analysis-vs-technical-analysis.html
12) http://www.markets.com/education/fundamental-analysis/what-is-fundamental-analysis.html

13) http://accountingexplained.com/financial/ratios/advantages-limitations

14) Saurav Dutta, Tony Griffin, Karen L. Jett, Jan Kooiman, Lon Petro, Siaw-Peng Wan (2009) – CMA Learning System Part 2: Financial Decision Making, Version 3.0, Institute of Management Accountants (IMA).

15) Brian Hock, Lynn Roden, David Fairchild (2010) – Part 2 Financial Decision Making, Hock International.

FUNDAMENTAL ANALYSIS OR TECHNICAL ANALYSIS

Fundamental Analysis seeks to understand the value of a share based on the intrinsic value of the company by focusing on the underlying factors that affect the company's operations as well as the forces operating in the economy. The future prospects of the company are also to be taken into consideration. This means that the entire economic structure of the company and the economy are taken into consideration. A lot of questions are answered such as the earnings potential, actual profits from operations, ability to repay debts, liquidity position of the company etc are all answered in Fundamental Analysis. Even window dressing, if done, can be analyzed through Fundamental Analysis. Hundreds of other questions can be answered through Fundamental Analysis. Fundamental Analysis is capable of finding out the true value of the company taking into consideration all the fundamentals of the company as well as the economic forces that affect the company. However, for this to happen, the investor needs to wait for a certain time and bear the ups and downs in the price of the company and wait for the price to reflect the true value of the company.

Technical Analysis only reflects the analysis of the investments based on price and volume through the use of various charts and other tools. They base their analysis on the prevailing sentiment in the market that is known as momentum. To be a Technical Analyst, one need not have any knowledge about the commodity. One has to only understand the chart and make a decision as to whether the signal being given is a buy, hold or a sell. Technical Analysis is based on the law of supply and demand. In case there is demand for a stock, the volume and price will reflect that and prices are predicted to go up whereas when the demand for a stock falls, this is reflected in the price of the stock and the price is expected to fall. Even when the Fundamental indicators of a company are strong, there is no guarantee of change in price of the company, especially in the short term. There is no measurement of the intrinsic value of a stock as the belief is that the fundamentals are reflected in the price prevailing in the market.

It is therefore evident that Fundamental looks not only on past performance of the stock but to the future prospects as well whereas Technical Analysis only takes into account the past history of the stock price and does not take into account any other data when evaluating a stock. Even if it is said that Technical Analysis takes into consideration all the Fundamentals of the stock, the data may be reflected totally very late to screen for potential investments.

Technical Analysis does not attempt to understand the underlying factors of a company being analyzed such as the products of the organization, the quality of the company, the research and development, the products being developed and other factors that affect the fundamentals of the company. In order to make a long term investment decision, such factors are extremely essential as they critically affect the true value of the stock. A Technical Analyst will ignore these factors and only track the technical indicators and patterns relating to the stock. Such information, at times has proved to be either unreliable or inaccurate.

Fundamental Analysis covers both, quantitative as well as qualitative analysis. The ratios that are calculated give the quantitative element in order to have objective comparison, not only with past results of the company itself but also with the industry as well as the sector as a whole. The qualitative analysis comes when the quantitative analysis is done. The analysis of whether the company is a good investment or not is based not on any individual number but taking together all the numbers as a whole. One of the major strengths of Fundamental Analysis is that the Efficient Markets Theory suggests that in the long run, the markets reflect the fundamentals of the company in the stock price. This means that all present and past data is reflected in the price.

In Technical Analysis, the market reflects rumors and expectations based on investor sentiment. Technical Analysts claim that all the things that will affect the price of the stock are included in the price chart. There are times that there are rumors in the market and there is a lot of noise in the market, a bullish trend will tend to take prices higher without being reflected by the fundamentals. Similarly, a bearish trend in the markets may cause the price of the stock of a company to fall while the fundamentals of the company are strong. Thus, the short term movement in price is not reflected by the fundamentals resulting in volatility in the share price and the markets in general. The belief in the markets is that if Technical Analysis works then validity of the Efficient Market Theory is in doubt.

Fundamental Analysis takes a long term approach (sometimes years) to investing whereas Technical Analysis takes a short term approach. The approach of technical analysis can be measured in a time frame of days, weeks and at times, even minutes. The fundamental analyst uses figures that are available over a long period of time. Financial statements used in Fundamental Analysis are made available only after certain time intervals whereas the technical analyst has information available on a daily basis. One of the reasons for using data over a long term period is that sometimes, it takes a long time for the fundamentals of the company to be reflected in the stock price. For a fundamental analyst, the intrinsic value may not be reflected in the stock price. This is also known as value investing. Value Investing is based on the principle that short term trading is not the correct way of investing. Value Investing makes an assumption that in the long run, the price of a stock will reflect the intrinsic value.

There are companies that are undervalued or overvalued in the market. Undervalued stocks represent an investment opportunity as the stock is cheaply available but the prospects of the company are bright as the earnings are not reflected fully in the share price. With time, the market price of such a stock will increase and thus, the investor will earn handsomely through capital appreciation as well as through dividends as and when they are declared. Overvalued stocks are stocks that are valued at high prices but the fundamentals of the stock are not strong. This means that the price of the stock in the market will likely fall and the investor may not be able to get a return on investment and may instead stand to lose a lot of money. Identifying such overvalued or undervalued stocks is possible with Fundamental Analysis. Technical Analysis will very likely ignore this aspect.

The goal of both, Fundamental and Technical Analysis is different. The goal of Technical Analysis is to trade. Traders buy shares with the goal of selling them at a higher price and making a profit. The goal of Fundamental Analysis is to invest. The goal of investment is to buy stocks that will increase in value.

The personality of the trader also has to be taken into account while choosing a method of Analysis. Some people have a strong preference for one method of analysis over the other. However, it must be said that for an ordinary investor who invests his/her life savings, Fundamental Analysis is a better way to understand stocks as he/she would prefer to know the value of the company and the money invested is for a medium to long period of time. These investors also prefer to have gains in the form of dividend and capital gains over a medium to long term.

For a trader who invests in the stock market on a daily basis and invests in a number of stocks across industries, to understand the day to day movements of the prices of these stocks and to trade daily, Technical Analysis is usually the preferred mode of analysis as the time involved in analysis is less and instant decisions can be made.

Based on the above, it is evident that Fundamental Analysis has a more wide spread reach in terms of analysis rather than Technical Analysis which keeps a narrow focus. Taking into consideration the time horizon for which the analysis is to be made, Fundamental Analysis is better for the long run whereas Technical Analysis is much more effective in the short run due to the volatility in the markets. Both Analyses are required to make an informed decision.

Fundamental Analysis has given investors better returns over the years as compared to Technical Analysis. Success stories are abundant where Fundamental Analysis is used. Famous investors such as Ramdeo Agarwal, Warren Buffet, Peter Lynch and Ramesh Damani made money in the stock markets with the used of Fundamental Analysis for making investment decisions.

REFERENCES:

1) http://www.slideshare.net/michaelkleven5/fundamental-analysisvstechnicalanalysis
2) http://www.extraordinaryinvestor.com/fundamental-analysis-benefits.html

A SOLVED EXAMPLE - ANALYSIS OF INTERNATIONAL POWER

ABOUT INTERNATIONAL POWER:

Company profile:

Formed in October 2000, by the demerger of National Power, International Power is a electricity generating company which generates electricity from gas, oil, coal, and renewable energy sources. Other complementary activities are undertaken for maximisation of profits. These include mining, coal and transporting gas by pipeline in Australia, desalinating water in the Middle East and providing steam for district heating systems in Europe. Some of the power sold was also through competitive merchant markets. The remainder is sold to single customers under long term power purchase agreements. The company is also interested in Environmental care, which forms an integral part of its operations. New initiatives range from developing the company's first wind farm in Australia to increasing the capability to burn more environmentally friendly fuels in U.K. coal – fired power station. Since the demerger, the company has increased international presence by building new generating assets in U.S., Oman, and the UAE and through the acquisition of plants in Australia, UAE and U.K.. The company aims to create value generation through managing existing asset portfolio efficiently, trading output competitively and growing the business in the core regions of North America, Europe, Middle East, and Australia. It also aims to maintain a balanced portfolio of assets in terms of fuel diversity, dispatch type, geographical spread and participation in both merchant markets and long term contracts. The company operates in a capital intensive industry requiring maximum plant capacity, and growth is acquired mainly through mergers and acquisitions. Long term success is dependant on the development opportunities secured. The company has a diverse portfolio, generating enough power to light up nearly 20 million homes. (Annual Report for 2003 of International Power, Pgs. 1-4, 11). The Group operates from corporate offices in London and Swindon, where corporate and business functions are based to support worldwide operations. In addition, the group operates regional business support offices in Australia, U.S., Czech Republic, Italy, Japan and the UAE. The offices vary in sizes depending on the operations in the region and apart from Australia and U.S. are primarily focussed on business development. (Annual Report for 2003 of International Power, Pgs. 1-4, 11)

FINANCIAL POSITION OF THE COMPANY:

Consolidated balance sheet

AT 31 DECEMBER 2004   Group

		31 December 2004	31 December 2003
			(restated)
Note		£m	£m
	Fixed assets		
	Intangible fixed assets:		
13	Goodwill	**8**	7
13	Negative goodwill	**(6)**	(6)
	Net goodwill	**2**	1
14	Tangible fixed assets	**3,654**	2,048
15	:		
	Share of gross assets	**642**	337
	Share of gross liabilities	**(330)**	(211)
	Net investment	**312**	126

	Associates	**853**	315
	Other investments	**86**	95
	Total fixed asset investments	**1,251**	536
	Total fixed assets	**4,907**	2,585
	Current assets		
16	Stocks	**87**	65
17	Debtors: amounts falling due within one year	**234**	157
	Debtors: amounts falling due after more than one year	**581**	3
	Total debtors	**815**	160
18	Investments	**201**	70
	Cash at bank and in hand	**411**	673
	Total current assets	**1,514**	968
19	**Creditors: amounts falling due within one year:**		
	Secured bank loans	**(71)**	(531)
	Other current liabilities (including convertible debt)	**(500)**	(315)

Creditors: amounts falling due within one year	**(571)**	(846)
Net current assets	**943**	122
Total assets less current liabilities	**5,850**	2,707
Creditors: amounts falling due after more than one year (including		
20 **convertible debt)**	**(3,384)**	(909)
21 **Provisions for liabilities and charges**	**(404)**	(238)
1 **Net assets**	**2,062**	1,560
Capital and reserves		
23/24 Called up share capital	**737**	554
24 Share premium account	**392**	289
24 Capital redemption reserve	**145**	145
24 Capital reserve	**422**	422
24 Profit and loss account	**129**	111
24 **Shareholders' funds – equity**	**1,825**	1,521
Minority interests – equity	**237**	39
Total equity	**2,062**	1,560

Consolidated profit and loss account

FOR THE YEAR ENDED 31 DECEMBER 2004

Note		**Excluding exceptional items** £m	**Exceptional items** £m	**Including exceptional items** £m	Excluding exceptional items £m	Exceptional items £m	Including exceptional items £m
		Year ended 31 December 2004			Year ended 31 December 2003		
1	Turnover: Group and share of joint ventures and associates	**1,267**	**–**	**1,267**	1,273	–	1,273
	Less: share of joint ventures' turnover	**(144)**	**–**	**(144)**	(136)	–	(136)
	Less: share of associates' turnover	**(355)**	**–**	**(355)**	(285)	–	(285)
1	**Group turnover**	**768**	**–**	**768**	852	–	852
	From continuing operations	**711**	**–**	**711**	852	–	852
	From acquisitions	**57**	**–**	**57**	–	–	–

2/8	Net operating costs	**(658)**	**11**	**(647)**	(727)	(404)	(1,131)
2	**Operating profit/(loss)**	**110**	**11**	**121**	125	(404)	(279)
	From continuing operations	**94**	**11**	**105**	125	(404)	(279)
	From acquisitions	**16**	**–**	**16**	–	–	–
	Share of operating profit of:						
	Joint ventures	**39**	**–**	**39**	32	–	32
8	Associates	**138**	**–**	**138**	95	35	130
	Income from investments	**–**	**–**	**–**	33	–	33
1/8	**Operating profit/(loss) and investment income**	**287**	**11**	**298**	285	(369)	(84)
8	Non-operating exceptional items:						
	Profit on sale of fixed asset investments	**–**	**4**	**4**	–	27	27
1	**Profit/(loss) on ordinary activities before interest and taxation**	**287**	**15**	**302**	285	(342)	(57)

4	Interest receivable and similar income	30	–	30	42	–	42
5/8	Interest payable and similar charges	(107)	(31)	(138)	(121)	(16)	(137)
5	Share of net interest of joint ventures and associates	(46)	–	(46)	(32)	–	(32)
	Net interest	(123)	(31)	(154)	(111)	(16)	(127)
3	**Profit/(loss) on ordinary activities before taxation**	164	(16)	148	174	(358)	(184)
8/9	Tax (charge)/credit on profit/(loss) on ordinary activities	(45)	–	(45)	(54)	26	(28)
	Profit/(loss) on ordinary activities after taxation	119	(16)	103	120	(332)	(212)
	Minority interests – equity	(11)	2	(9)	(7)	–	(7)
	Profit/(loss) for the financial year	108	(14)	94	113	(332)	(219)
10	Dividends	(37)	–	(37)	–	–	–
	Retained profit/(loss)	71	(14)	57	113	(332)	(219)
12	**Earnings/(loss) per share:**						
	Basic	**8.3p**		**7.2p**	9.1p		(17.6)p
	Diluted	**8.2p**		**7.1p**	9.0p		(17.6)p

SOME KEY FINANCIAL RATIOS:

Group ratios from the consolidated Profit and Loss Account for the year ended 31/12/2004 and Balance Sheet as at 31/12/2004 taken from the Annual Accounts of the company from the website www. Investis.com

(All figures are in Millions)

1. LIQUIDITY RATIOS:
a. Current Ratio: Current Assets

$$\text{Current Liabilities}$$

$$(2004) \qquad = \frac{1514}{1142}$$

$$= 1.325 \text{ times}$$

$$(2003) \qquad = \frac{968}{1692}$$

$$= 0.572 \text{ times}$$

The current ratio indicates the solvency of the company. As compared to 2003, in 2004, the current ratio of the company has decreased.

b. Quick Ratio: Current Assets – Stock

$$\text{Current Liabilities}$$

$$(2004) \qquad = \frac{1514 - 87}{1147}$$

$$= \frac{11427}{1142}$$

$$= 1.249 \text{ times}$$

$$(2003) \qquad = \frac{968\text{-}65}{}$$

1692

$$= \underline{903}$$

1692

$$= 0.5336 \text{ times}$$

This ratio indicates the immediate solvency of the company. It indicates liquidity. The decrease in this ratio is due to increase in the Sundry Creditors of the company.

2. ASSET MANAGEMENT RATIOS:

a. Inventory Turnover Ratio: Sales

Inventories

$$(2004) \qquad = \underline{768}$$

87

$$= 8.827 \text{ times}$$

$$(2003) \qquad = \underline{852}$$

65

$$= 13.107 \text{ times}$$

Industry turnover ratio indicates the inventory being converted into sales. This ratio has effect on the profitability of the firm .A low turnover ratio means that inventory level of the firm is higher than average. As the inventory of the company has increased in 2004 as compared to 2003 and sales have fallen the ratio is currently unfavourable as compared to the past performance of the company.

b. Days Sales Outstanding: Receivables

Average Sales Per Day

(2004)	= $\underline{815}$
	(768/365)
	= 387.357 days

(2003)	= $\underline{160}$
	(852/365)
—	= 68.55 days

This ratio analyses the credit policy of the firm. If the days sales outstanding ratio is high , then the company may have to examine the debt collection policy. It may also indicate that the debtors are not paying debts promptly and may lead to bad debt. The average collection days increased dramatically in 2004 as compared to 2003. This indicates that the company's credit policy has declined and the company needs to restructure its policy. The company also has to see the total bad debt it has incurred.

In comparison to this the payments to creditors has quickened since the last year. This has resulted in a Working Capital gap.

c. Fixed Asset Turnover Ratio (Evaluating Fixed Assets):   Sales

Fixed Assets

(2004)   = $\underline{768}$

4907

=

0.156 times

(2003)   = $\underline{852}$

2585

=

0.329 times

This indicates the intensity of the use of the fixed assets. As compared to 2003, the intensity of use has fallen. However, this may be due to the fact that the company has acquired the assets of another company , leading to excess capacity which has not been utilised and which may be done so in the future.

d. Total Assets Ratio (Evaluating Total Assets):   Sales

Total Assets

(2004)   = 768

6421

= 0.1196 times

(2003)   = 852

3553

= 0.2397 times

This ratio indicates how efficiently the assets of the company are being used by the company to increase the sales of the company in order to achieve higher profitability. As compared to 2003 the figures for 2004 are lower. However, this maybe due to the fact that the company has acquired the assets of another company and the ratio may show an increase in the future. The company has also impaired an asset. This can also lead to a lower ratio in the current year. This ratio indicates a high degree of capital intensity.

3. DEBT EQUITY MANAGEMENT RATIOS:

a.   Debt Equity Ratio: Total Long Term Debts
                                         Net Worth

(2004)   = 4526

6421

= 0.704 times   =2.20 times

(2003) $= \dfrac{2601}{3553}$

= 0.7320 times   =0.58 times

The creditors of a company usually look closely at this ratio. They prefer a low ratio as it indicates a higher degree of protection if bankruptcy occurs. This ratio of the company has declined showing that the creditors of the company are well protected as against the previous year.

The Total Debt to Equity ratio takes into account both long-term and short-term debt. Traditionally, one would analyze a company's leverage on the basis of its long-term debt, which includes debt that is due more than one year hence. Long-Term Debt is assumed to be a permanent part of the company's capital structure. Short-term debt is traditionally regarded as not being part of the capital structure. With trade debt, for example, a manufacturer might borrow money to finance the purchase of raw material, which is converted into finished products and sold to customers. Once the company receives the proceeds of these sales, it immediately repays the money it borrowed in order to finance its raw material purchases. Such debt is not usually regarded   as   part   of   the   company's   capital   base.

But nowadays, borrowing arrangements have become much more flexible. Many companies use short-term debt as if it was part of the capital structure. This occurs when companies continually refinance the debt as soon as it comes due. This might be done if a company expects interest rates to fall. Continually refinancing short-term debts at lower and lower interest rates is preferable to locking the company into a long-term obligation at an interest rate that will be well above   rates   that   are   likely   to   prevail   in   the   marketplace   next   year. During the year the company has raised substantial equity as well as debt. Debt equity Ratio of the company as a result has now become almost fully exhausted leaving very little for raising additional long term funds.

The Fixed Assets to Capital employed is extremely high. Given the nature of business, a high Fixed Assets to Capital Employed ratio, although acceptable, does not justify the ratio in excess of 1(one). This means that the company has used short term funds to create Long term assets. A practice   which   could   prove   extremely   dangerous. This strategy can be risky. If the company's interest rate forecast proves wrong, its cost structure will suffer. It may wind up refinancing its short-term debt at a rate that is well above the rate it might have paid had it borrowed long-term in the first place. Either way, we suggest looking at total debt/equity as an additional measure of financial leverage as well. When doing so, consider two issues:

The more debt in a company's capital structure, the greater the financial leverage risk. If business turns weak, there are some costs a company can easily reduce to protect its profits and preserve liquidity. But interest on debt is generally not among these variable costs. Interest must be paid even when revenues are falling. Hefty levels of debt and heavy interest expense burdens could led to insolvency if revenues or operating profits remain weak for a prolonged   period.

The larger the Total Debt to Equity Ratio is relative to the LT Debt to Equity Ratio, the more risk the company faces from the prospect of rising interest rates. But remember, some short-term debt is based on a corporate forecast of lower interest rates, while other types of short-term debt represents trade borrowing, such as the above raw materials financing example. You can't always tell for certain what sort of short-term debt your company has. But you can make some reasonable assumptions by using the Reuters Report to compare your company's debt ratios with those of its industry peers. A company that uses short-term debt much more aggressively than others in its industry is probably doing so because it expects lower interest rates.

It is generally assumed that higher debt ratios signify greater levels of risk. But don't jump too quickly to conclusions. Companies in industries characterized by stable cash flows can safely carry more debt than can companies whose cash flows follow volatile trends. Before you reach your final conclusion, you will need to compare the company's ratios with those of its industry peers. Look, too, at the final part of the Financial Strength Ratio Comparisons Report, which shows Interest Coverage. Companies with high levels of interest coverage are better   able   to   carry   more   debt.

Since debt increases risk, why should any company ever carry any debt? Wouldn't it be reasonable   to   simply   restrict   consideration   to   debt-free   companies?

There are two reasons why you should not narrow your horizons this way. First, as discussed above, some forms of debt, such as trade debt, are necessary to the day-to-day operation of a business. This is especially so in the financial sector, where much depends on the process of borrowing money and re-lending it at higher rates. Second, permanent debt, prudently used, can enhance corporate returns. You can measure this effect by examining the Management Effectiveness table.(http://www.investor.reuters.com/learn.aspx?ticker=IPR.N&target=%2fstocks%2ffinancialinfo%2fratios%2ffinancialcondition&page=learn)

b. Total Interest Earned: Earnings before interest and taxes(EBIT)
                                    Interest Charges

    (2004)   =   321 = 1.745 times

184

=   (where profit excludes exceptional items)

= $\dfrac{332}{184}$ = 1.804 times

=   (where profit includes exceptional items)

(2003)   = $\dfrac{389}{169}$ = 2.301 times

=   (where profit excludes exceptional items)

= $\dfrac{-15}{169}$ = -0.0887 times   (where profit includes exceptional items)

The interest coverage ratio is poor, in case where effect of exceptional items are removed.

c. Debt Capitalisation Ratio:

         (2004)   133%

         (2003)   44%

4. PROFITABILITY RATIOS:

a. Profit Margin on Sales: $\dfrac{\text{Net Income to Common Shareholders}}{\text{Common Eqiuty}}$

(2004) $= \dfrac{108}{768}$

= 0.1406

= 14.06%

(2003) $= \underline{113}$

$$852$$

$$= 0.1326$$

$$= 13.26\%$$

The net income to common shareholders has increased as compared to 2003 in 2004. as the common equity has fallen. But the profitability of the company has also fallen as compared to the previous year. The company should examine its costs. This maybe due to the acquisition and also the impairment of the asset.

The company's turnover has gone down and the profitability as compared to the previous year after adjusting the extraordinary item has also declined. The Net Profit margin before the extraordinary item has almost become half as compared to the previous year. However, due to a profit appearing in the books, the company has decided to declare a dividend thereby reducing its retained profit margin even further.

b. Return to Common Eqiuty: Net Income available to Shareholders

$$\text{Common Equity}$$

(2004)
$$= \frac{108}{2062}$$

$$= 0.0523$$

$$= 5.235\% \; (\text{ where net income excludes exceptional items })$$

$$= \frac{94}{2062}$$

$$= 0.0455$$

$$= 4.55\% \; (\text{ where net income includes exceptional items })$$

(2003)
$$= \frac{113}{554}$$

$$= 0.2039$$

$$= 20.39\% \; (\text{ where net income excludes exceptional items })$$

$$= \frac{-219}{554}$$

$$= -0.257$$

$$= -25.7\% \quad \text{(where net income includes exceptional items)}$$

This ratio is more important from the shareholders point of view. This ratio indicates the profit that is earned by the shareholders after charges have been met. When exceptional items have been excluded, the profitability of the firm has increased dramatically from 2003 in 2004. This indicates to the shareholders that the company is performing well and that they will get adequate returns on their investments.

5. MARKET VALUE RATIOS:

a. Earnings per share: Given in Consolidated Profit and Loss Account. Both figures have been adjusted for the rights issue.

b. Dividend Cover: $\dfrac{\text{Earnings per share}}{\text{Annual Dividend per share}}$

(2004) $= \dfrac{8.3}{(37/2062)}$

= 463.687 times (in case of basic EPS excluding   exceptional items)

$= \dfrac{7.2}{0.0179}$

= 402.234 times (in case of basic EPS with exceptional items)

$= \dfrac{8.2}{0.0179}$

= 458.100 times (in case of diluted EPS excluding ecceptional items)

$= \dfrac{7.1}{0.0179}$

= 396.648 times (in case of diluted EPS including exceptional items)

(2003)   = No dividend has been declared for the financial year ending on 31/12/2003

c. Price Earnings Ratio: Current Market Price per Equity Share

                     Earnings per share

This ratio is the single most widely used measure of a stock's value. That's because the key to stock ownership is the shareholder's stake in a portion of the company's profit stream (http://www.investor.reuters.com)

d. Return on Equity: Profit after tax and preference dividend

                     Equity Capital and Reserves

(2004) $= \dfrac{108}{2062}$

             = 0.0523

             = 5.23% (where profit excludes exceptional items)

             $= \dfrac{94}{2062}$

             = 0.0455

             = 4.55% (where profit includes exceptional items)

(2003) $= \dfrac{113}{976}$

             = 0.1157 (where profit excludes exceptional items)

             $= \dfrac{-219}{976}$

             = 0.224 (where profit includes exceptional items)

This ratio indicates how much profit is available for distribution as dividend after payment of tax and preference dividend. The ratio has improved a lot in 2004 as compared to 2003 indicating a better return on investment for the shareholders and also indicates higher profitability which indicates growth of the company.

e. Return on capital employed: <u>Profit before interest and tax</u>

Total Assets – Current Liablilties

(2004) $= \dfrac{287}{571}$

$= 0.5026$

$= 50.26\%$ (where profit is calculated excluding exceptional items)

$= \dfrac{302}{571}$

$= 0.5144$

$= 51.44 \%$ (where profit includes exceptional items)

(2003) $= \dfrac{285}{3553}$

$= 0.0802$

$= 8.02 \%$ (where profit is calculated excluding exceptional items)

$= \dfrac{-57}{3553}$

$=- 0.1604$

$=- 16.04\%$ (where profit includes exceptional items)

This ratio shows the total company performance in the form of a return on the assets employed available to all the sources of finance. This ratio has shown dramatic improvement as compared to 2003 indicating that there is enough return on investment to pay all the sources of finance as well as indicates higher profitability and growth.

f. Gearing Ratio:

(2005)   133%
(2003)   44%
(http://www.investis.com)

 All the above factors points to the necessity for a quick infusion of equity capital in the company without which the company may face substantial liquidity problems which will hamper its growth in the future.

MERGERS AND ACQUISITIONS:

Firstly, International Power acquired the international generating assets of Edison Mission Energy (EME). This portfolio comprises nine assets in six countries with a net generating capacity of 3,202 MW, representing a significant increase in our total capacity. This was a major acquisition, costing some US$1.9 billion (£972 million), undertaken in a 70:30 partnership with Mitsui of Japan, who are well known through previous joint developments in Asia and the Middle East.. The EME assets are an excellent fit, with seven of the nine assets having secure long-term contracts, and the other two operating in our core merchant markets of the UK and Victoria (Australia). These assets are now being quickly and successfully integrated into the existing regional structure, giving an immediate and significant increase in earnings.

Secondly, International Power completed the acquisition of a majority stake in Turbogás in Portugal, a modern and efficient 990 MW gas fired plant. This asset, together with the existing investment in Portugal – namely the 600 MW Pego coal fired plant – provides a profitable, cash generative and highly integrated Portuguese portfolio, and positions International Power very well for the anticipated liberalisation of the Iberian market.

Thirdly, the restructuring of the US$879 million (£488 million) non-recourse debt facility for our US merchant portfolio was completed. As International Power flagged last year, the low margins in our US merchant markets resulted in insufficient cash flow to fully meet interest costs. After carefully evaluating all options , it was concluded that it was in the best interests of shareholders to retain the upside exposure to the medium-term recovery in our US markets. The restructured facility, extended to 2010, provides a solid capital structure, and International Power can now fully concentrate on ways of commercially strengthening our US business.

Throughout these major moves, there was a major element of the Group cash reserves and assuming a significant amount of non-recourse debt, focus was kept on maintaining a prudent capital structure. The objective was to add no additional debt at the Group centre, and to retain some capacity to execute value–added growth opportunities in our core regions. It was concluded that a Rights Issue was the most appropriate option.(Chief Executive Officer's Statement, http://www.investis.com/ip/reports/ar2004/content/ceo.html)

On 17 December 2004, acquisition of nine of the international generation assets of the EME portfolio in a 70:30 partnership with Mitsui (IPM) was concluded. The existing shareholder at CBK (Philippines) has exercised pre–emption rights, and at Doga (Turkey) the required shareholder consent has not been obtained. In addition, existing shareholders at Italian Wind (Italy) and Tri Energy (Thailand) have exercised a 'right of purchase' and these assets will not form part of International Power's portfolio.

As a result of these events, International Power will own 3,202 MW (net), representing 85% of the EME portfolio. The net cash consideration will be reduced by US$339 million (£178 million) from the expected net cash consideration of US$2.2 billion (£1.15 billion) for the entire EME portfolio. In summary the loss of these assets has no material impact on either the overall returns or the commercial rationale of the acquisition. Following the disposal of Italian Wind, and after accounting for all costs associated with the acquisition, our 70% interest resulted in a cash outflow of some £375 million, with the remainder of the acquisition price funded by Mitsui and bank finance.

Going forward, the EME portfolio consists of nine power generation projects in six countries. These assets complement our existing portfolio by adding quality assets in our core markets, particularly Australia, Europe and Asia.

The portfolio is strongly contracted, with seven of the projects under long-term PPAs and hedge contracts. The two assets that operate on a merchant basis, First Hydro and Valley Power, fit very well into existing portfolio in core markets of the UK and Australia.

The IPM partnership benefits from International Power and Mitsui's complementary strategies and skills. Both companies are committed to a long-term partnership to deliver maximum value from the acquisition. International Power has previously worked with Mitsui on international projects in the Middle East and Pakistan for over ten years. Mitsui has extensive experience in the Asian market (they already own a 36.6% shareholding in Paiton) as well as world–class power generation, engineering, procurement and construction skills. These newly acquired assets are now integrated and managed in the International Power regional structure.

Including the assets acquired from the EME portfolio, which added 884 MW (net) of new capacity, International Power's generation capacity in Australia now totals 3,275 MW (net). This enhanced capacity has increased the Company's share of the Australian national electricity market to circa 12%, up from 8% before the EME acquisition. This represents a market share of some 27% in Victoria and 20% in South Australia.

The integration of the EME assets is well advanced and good progress has been made on extracting synergies in a number of business areas including trading, settlement, regional office and business development. Relevant management structures are now in place and selected staff members from EME have been integrated within the International Power team. EME's Melbourne office is in the process of being closed(http://www.investis.com/ip/reports/ar2004/content/operating)

EXCEPTIONAL ITEMS:

During the year , the group recorded two operating exceptional items:

2)   impairment of the US plant by £404 million
3)   reversal of past impairment of HUBCO investment

The carrying values of the US plant were reviewed , following the sharp decline in both current and forward electricity prices in the ERCOT and NEPOOOL markets in the US. This resulted in the impairment of the US merchant plants(Hays, Midlothian, Blackstone,Bellingham and Milford). The revised US book values were determined by applying a risk adjusted discount rate of 9.7% to the post-tax cash flows expected from the plants over their remaining useful lives. Additionally during the year, the Group recorded the following three non-operating exceptional items:

• profit on disposal of a 5% holding in HUBCO

of £17 million;

• profit on disposal of a Czech fixed asset investment

of £7 million;

• proceeds and a gain relating to China exit of £3 million.

NET INTEREST:

Net interest payable for the year ended 31 December 2003 was £111 million (excluding exceptional items). Corporate and subsidiary operations accounted for interest payable of £79 million comprising gross interest of £123 million on bonds, bank loans and overdrafts offset by £23 million interest receivable, foreign exchange gains of £19 million and by capitalised interest of £2 million. Associates and joint ventures incurred net interest payable of £32 million.

Consolidated interest cover was 2.6 times (excluding exceptional items). Additionally during 2003, the Group recorded an exceptional interest charge of £16 million in relation to the write-off of unamortised facility costs in the US and the UK.

TAX:

The tax charge for the year (pre-exceptional items) amounted to £54 million compared to £77 million in the previous year. The tax charge represents an effective tax rate of 31%, compared to 30% in the prior period. Additionally during 2003, the Group recorded an exceptional tax credit of £26 million relating to a net write back of deferred tax following the impairment of the US plant.

We are (2003actively seeking viable renewable energy opportunities for future development.

Above: Pego, Tejo Energia Portugal

(2003)(13)

MY POSITION ON WHETHER TO BUY OR SELL THE STOCK:

Based on analyst opinion given below and also on the basis of the key ratios of the company , I would buy the stock of the company. The company is in a healthy financial position. It's ratios have also improved in the year ending 2004 as compared to the year ending 2003. Besides, it has also acquired a new plant and is currently expanding. It had also made a bid for the British power utility Drax, which indicates that the company is earning profits and has sufficiently large reserves. The liquidity ratios of the company have also substantially improved. The gearing ratio and the market capitalisation ratio has also improved. Returns to shareholders have also increased. In the year ending 2004, the company also declared a dividend of 2.5p per share indicating return to investors.   The return on capital employed has also increased, suggesting a increased return on capital employed, which indicates more efficient use of capital. The dividend cover has also increased from 2003 in 2004 suggesting that more dividend would be available to the shareholders.   The return to common equity ratio also improved in 2004 as compared to 2003, indicating that morte income was available to the shareholders to be distributed as dividend which also indicates higher profitability. The company is rapidly expanding and the analyst opinion is also to buy the stock. In my opinion, the stock is a good buy and is worth adding to the portfolio. This company will give consistent performance in the future period with the rate at whuch it is growing. Even in 2005, the company is acquiring additional assets, improving its capabilities to expand in the future. It is already one of the leading players in the industry which indicates good profitability and adequate returns for the investors.

CURRENT NEWS :

International Power had made a bid for Britain's Drax Power Station, but dropped out as per the information given by Reuters on November 8, 2005.

May 31 (Bloomberg) -- International Power Plc, an electricity producer on four continents, and Japanese trading company Mitsui & Co. will pay U.S.-based Calpine Corp. 490 million pounds ($889 million) for its Saltend plant in the U.K.

International Power will have a 70 percent stake and Mitsui 30 percent in the 1,200-megawatt Saltend Energy Centre, Mitsui said today in a statement to the Tokyo Stock Exchange. Calpine, which owns power plants in 21 states, put its largest generator up for sale in January. (http://www.bloomberg.com)

COMPETITORS:

Top Competitors

- AES
- Mirant

SUEZ-TRACTEBEL

(http://www.hoovers.com)

SOME FINANCIAL HIGHLIGHTS AND COMPARISON WITH COMPETITORS ALONG WITH ANALYST OPINION:

Financial Highlights

Fiscal Year End:	December
Revenue (2004):	1472.00 M
Revenue Growth (1 yr):	(-3.10%)
Employees (2004):	2,750
Employee Growth (1 yr):	13.80%

(Figures in $)

(http://www.biz.yahoo.com/ic/47/47995.87)

IPR LSE 16:07 GMT
UK:IPR \boxed{\text{Create}} |

Create   News   alert   - Add to my portfolio
\boxed{\text{Add}}

Quotes	23Nov2005
Last	244.250 p
Change	▲ 3.25
% Change (1)	▲ **1.35%**
High	244.25
Open	242.50
Low	240.75
Net Volume	4,443,170

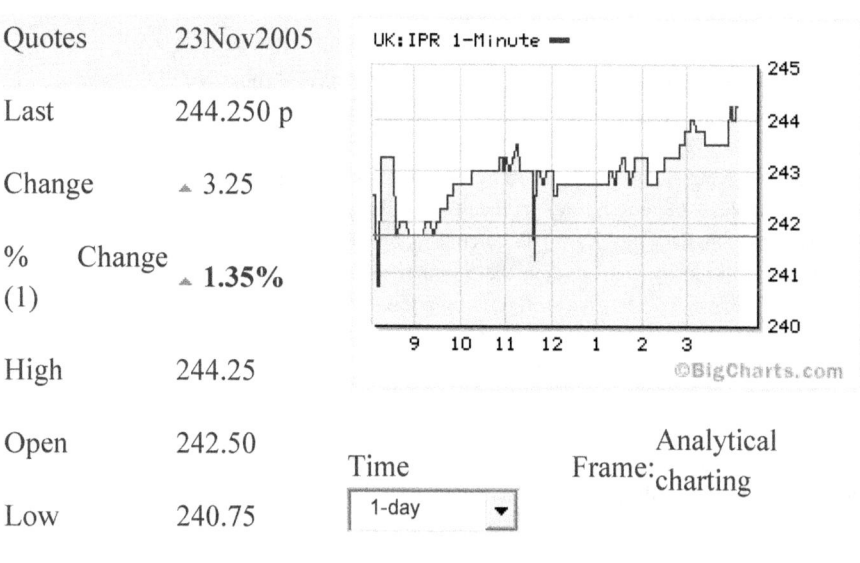

Time Frame: 1-day ▼

Analytical charting

Fundamentals

52 Wk High (2) Date	254.25 4/10/2005
52 Wk Low (3) Date	145.75 15/12/2004
Dividend	2.50
Div Date	25/5/2005
Market Cap (4)	3,599 M GBP

Last 5 days quote

Date	Close	Net Change	% Change **
22Nov2005	241	▼ -0.25	-0.10%
21Nov2005	241.25	▲ 4.00	1.69%
18Nov2005	237.25	▼ -3.50	-1.45%
17Nov2005	240.75	▼ -2.50	-1.03%
16Nov2005	243.25	▼ -0.25	-0.10%

P/E Ratio (5) 33.92

EPS (6)   7.20

(1) = %Change based on previous day close (2) (3) = 52 Week High and Low values are based on intraday values reached by a given security. (4) = Market Capitalisation is calculated by multiplying a given security's shares outstanding figure by the previous day's closing price. The shares outstanding figures include traded shares only. (5) = P/E Ratio (Price to Earnings Ratio) is calculated by taking the last price for a given security and dividing that number with the basic or adjusted EPS (Earnings per Share) figure reported directly by the company. (6) = EPS (Earnings per Share) value is taken from the basic or adjusted EPS figure reported directly by the company.

The share price of the company showed a steady increase indicating investor confidence in the company. In 2005 also, the company has shown better results indicating that the company is growing steadily.

Company Type	Public (London: IPR; NYSE: IPR [ADR])
Fiscal Year-End	December
2004 Sales (mil.)	£764.0
1-Year Sales Growth	(3.1%)
2004 Net Income (mil.)	£93.4
2004 Employees	2,750
1-Year Employee Growth	13.8%

(http://www.hoovers.com)

Industry: **Electricity**   Employees: **2,416** (12/31/2005)

Officers: Sir Neville Simms, Non Executive Chairman Philip Cox, Chief Executive Mark Williamson, Chief Financial Officer Stephen Ramsay, Secretary

Share Related Items		Dividend Information		Profitability	
Mkt. Cap. (Mil) $	**6,239.82**	Yield %	**0.00**	Gross Margin (TTM) %	**0.00**
Shares Out (Mil)	**147.34**	Annual Dividend	**0.00**		
		Payout Ratio (TTM) %	**0**	Operating Margin (TTM) %	**6.92**
				Profit Margin (TTM) %	**-25.70**

Valuation Ratios		Per Share Data		Mgmt Effectiveness	
Price/Earnings (TTM)	**17.07**	Earnings (TTM) $	**2.43**	Return on Equity (TTM)	**-12.86**
Price/Sales (TTM)	**5.36**	Sales (TTM) $	**7.91**		
Price/Book (MRQ) $	**1.77**	Book Value (MRQ) $	**23.58**	Return on Assets (TTM)	**-3.54**
Price/Cash Flow (TTM) $	**7.11**	Cash Flow (TTM) $	**3.41**	Return on Investment (TTM)	**-4.15**

Financial Strength

Quick Ratio (MRQ)   **1.11**   Current Ratio (MRQ)   **1.19**   LT Debt/Equity (MRQ)   **1.76**

Total Debt/Equity (MRQ)   **NA**

Mil = Millions MRQ = Most Recent Quarter TTM = Trailing Twelve Months

Financial Snapshot		Per-Share Estimates			Current Analyst Ratings	
	2003		This Fiscal	Next Fiscal	Strong Buy	**2**
					Moderate Buy	**1**
Revenue	**$ 1.4 B**					
Total Net Income	**$ -360.3 M**	Mean Estimate	**2.30**	**3.12**	Hold	**0**
Earnings Per Share	**$ -2.89**	High	**2.31**	**3.18**	Moderate Hold	**0**

EBITDA	$ -139.9 M	Estimates			Sell	0
Long Term Debt	$ 1.6 B	Low Estimates	2.28	3.06	Mean	**STRONG BUY**
More Financial Information		# of Estimates	2&	2	More Analyst Ratings	
		More Earnings Estimates				

(http://money.cnn.com)

All amounts in millions of British Pounds except share amounts

Year	Revenue	Gross Profit	Operating Income	Total Income	Net	Diluted Income)	EPS	(Net
Dec 04	764.0	180.1	54.0	180.0		0.71		
Dec 03	854.1	232.8	59.0	(390.0)		(1.97)		
Dec 02	719.9	271.8	74.2	182.0		1.02		

(http://www.hoovers.com)

Quarterly Income Statements

All amounts in millions of British Pounds except share amounts

Year	Revenue	Gross Profit	Operating Income	Total Income	Net	Diluted Income)	EPS	(Net

Mar 05	387.4	101.7	51.6	170.0	0.59
Dec 04	243.9	45.2	(22.8)	50.0	0.06
Sep 04	204.5	36.1	18.3	25.0	0.23
Jun 04	175.9	68.6	24.3	27.0	0.33
Mar 04	176.9	40.5	40.5	79.0	0.39

(http://www.hoovers.com)

All amounts in millions of British Pounds except share amounts

Year	Revenue	Gross Profit	Operating Income	Total Income	Net	Diluted EPS (Net Income)
Mar 05	387.4	101.7	51.6	170.0		0.59
Dec 04	243.9	45.2	(22.8)	50.0		0.06
Sep 04	204.5	36.1	18.3	25.0		0.23
Jun 04	175.9	68.6	24.3	27.0		0.33
Mar 04	176.9	40.5	40.5	79.0		0.39

(http://www.hoovers.com)

The revenue of the company has shown steady increase in each quarter. Steady growth indicates that the company is not a risky venture and that the company will continue to grow steadily in the future. This indicates that this is not a one time exceptional profit, but that this is a company which will show steady growth.

Comparison To Industry & Market

Valuation	Company	Industry[1]	Market[2]
Price/Sales Ratio	3.27	0.99	1.25
Price/Earnings Ratio	22.73	14.78	18.55
Price/Book Ratio	1.68	1.58	2.60
Price/Cash Flow Ratio	12.91	4.89	10.24

- [1]**Industry:** Foreign Utilities
- [2]**Market:** Public companies trading on the NYSE, AMEX, and NASDAQ

(http://www.hoovers.com/international-power/--ID__47995,ticker__--/free-co-fin-factsheet.xht)

As compared to the industry also, International Power is a very profitable company.

Top Competitors

	International Power	AES	Mirant	SUEZ-TRACTEBEL
Annual Sales	833.6	5,371.9	2,589.1	22,658.6
Employees	2,750	30,000	4,700	87,300
Market Cap ($ mil.)	3,490.9	5,881.3	0.0	0.0

(http://www.hoovers.com/international-power/--ID__47995,ticker__--/free-co-fin-factsheet.xht)

As compared to the competitors, International Power is very small in size, yet it has a good market capitalization ratio.

Data   News archive   Profiles   Financials

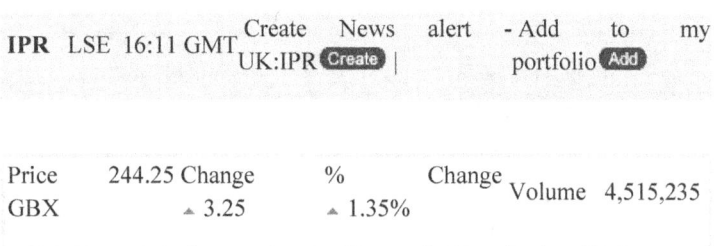

IPR LSE 16:11 GMT Create News alert - Add to my
UK:IPR Create | portfolio Add

| Price GBX | 244.25 ▲ 3.25 | Change | % ▲ 1.35% | Change | Volume | 4,515,235 |

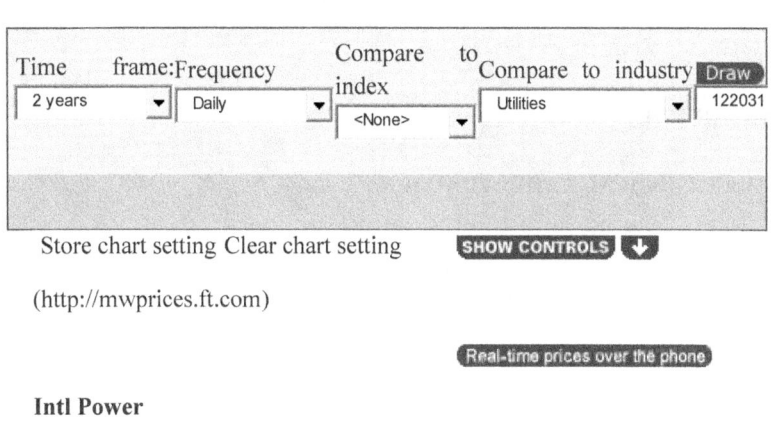

| Time | frame:Frequency | Compare to index | Compare to industry | Draw |
| 2 years ▼ | Daily ▼ | <None> ▼ | Utilities ▼ | 122031 |

Store chart setting Clear chart setting   SHOW CONTROLS ↓

(http://mwprices.ft.com)

    Real-time prices over the phone

Intl Power

| Data | News archive | Profiles | Financials |

Quotes | **Analytical charting** | Consensus forecast | Analyst reports | Annual reports

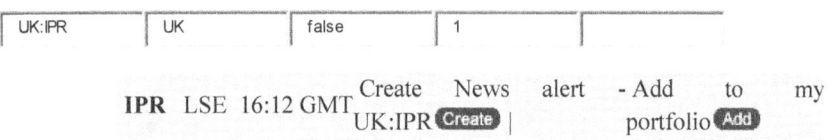

| UK:IPR | UK | false | 1 | |

IPR LSE 16:12 GMT Create News alert - Add to my
UK:IPR Create | portfolio Add

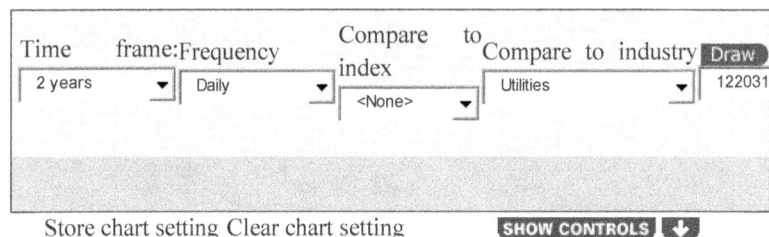

Price 244.25 Change % Change Volume 4,531,895
GBX ▲ 3.25 ▲ 1.35%

Time frame:	Frequency	Compare to index	Compare to industry	Draw
2 years ▼	Daily ▼	<None> ▼	Utilities ▼	122031

Store chart setting Clear chart setting SHOW CONTROLS ⬇

(http://mwprices.ft.com)

ANALYST OPINION:

UPGRADES & DOWNGRADES HISTORY

Date	Research Firm	Action	From	To
2-Nov-04	Lehman Brothers	Downgrade	Overweight	**Equal-weight**
2-Aug-04	JP Morgan	Upgrade	Underweight	**Neutral**
15-Jan-02	Salomon Smth Brny	Upgrade	Outperform	**Buy**

(Data provided by http://briefing.com)

COMPARISON WITH INDUSTRY:

COMPARISON WITH COMPARISON	IPR	AES	MIRKQ .PK	**Pvt1**	Industry

Market Cap:	61.69B	10.26B	494.67M	N/A	26.73B
Employees:	2,750	30,000	4,700	87,300[1]	2.75K
Qtrly Rev Growth (yoy):	174.90%	17.20%	-21.50%	N/A	18.80%
Revenue (ttm):	2.61B	9.87B	3.70B	40.01B[1]	5.49B
Gross Margin (ttm):	18.49%	29.27%	12.98%	N/A	37.86%
EBITDA (ttm):	1.04B	3.65B	518.00M	N/A	2.02B
Oper Margins (ttm):	18.68%	27.42%	4.68%	N/A	26.90%
Net Income (ttm):	288.46M	425.00M	-2.09B	N/A	369.25M
EPS (ttm):	0.191	0.721	-5.139	N/A	0.57
P/E (ttm):	217.38	21.79	N/Λ	N/A	38.26
PEG (5 yr expected):	0.63	1.17	N/A	N/A	2.74
P/S (ttm):	23.81	1.05	0.13	N/A	7.28

AES = AES Corp.

(Figures in $)

(http;//finance.yahoo.com)

The comparison with the industry and the direct competitors suggests that the net income of International Power is lesser than that of the industry average .It's operating margin and revenue are also well below the industry average as a result of which its EBIT is also well below the industry average. But International Power has a good market capitalisation ratio . The lower income is due to the fact that it is smaller in size than its direct competitors and employees lesser people. However, compared to its size and its assets, International Power is a highly profitable company which is expanding at a very rapid rate.

SHARE PRICES FOR THE YEAR 2004:

PRICES

Date	Open	High	Low	Close	Avg Vol	Adj Close*
Dec-04	29.76	30.75	29.43	30.55	4,890	30.13
Nov-04	30.09	31.00	28.51	29.51	5,985	29.10
Oct-04	26.57	30.10	26.57	30.00	6,647	29.59
8-Sep-04	$ 2.736 Cash Dividend					
Sep-04	27.60	27.60	24.80	26.55	5,757	26.18
Aug-04	26.87	27.73	25.98	27.46	2,400	24.34
Jul-04	25.71	27.59	24.90	27.31	1,761	24.20
Jun-04	27.00	27.30	25.62	25.75	2,580	22.82
May-04	25.10	27.10	24.55	26.75	2,470	23.71
Apr-04	27.25	28.60	25.10	25.10	2,600	22.24
Mar-04	26.41	27.05	24.30	27.05	2,469	23.97
Feb-04	22.80	26.60	22.80	26.40	5,284	23.40
Jan-04	22.37	24.65	22.14	22.27	875	19.74

* Close price adjusted for dividends and splits.

(http://finance.yahoo.com)

Share price in the year 2004 has also shown an increase, volume traded on the New York Stock exchange also increased, indicating market confidence in the company. The company also declared cash dividend in the year indicating that the company has made good profits during the year which increases the confidence of the shareholders in general that the company will perform well in the future.

INTERNATIONAL POWER COMPARED WITH THE INDUSTRY:

Valuation Ratios

RATIO COMPARISON

Valuation Ratios	Company	Industry	Sector	S&P 500
P/E Ratio (TTM)	16.55	18.39	19.01	20.77
P/E High - Last 5 Yrs.	NA	31.31	30.02	38.32
P/E Low - Last 5 Yrs.	NA	10.24	11.10	15.02
Beta	1.73	0.39	0.49	1.00
Price to Sales (TTM)	2.20	1.45	1.61	2.91
Price to Book (MRQ)	1.37	3.67	3.58	4.05
Price to Tangible Book (MRQ)	1.76	3.66	3.77	6.89
Price to Cash Flow (TTM)	9.33	8.96	10.35	15.07
Price to Free Cash Flow (TTM)	NM	21.07	25.21	28.17
% Owned Institutions	0.72	60.28	58.32	67.67

›Learn about Valuation Ratios

Dividends

Dividends	Company	Industry	Sector	S&P 500
Dividend Yield	1.05	3.67	3.54	2.08
Dividend Yield - 5 Year Avg.	0.00	4.05	3.97	1.63
Dividend 5 Year Growth Rate	-100.00	-5.69	-7.73	8.08
Payout Ratio (TTM)	0.00	55.36	51.73	27.96

›Learn about Dividend Ratios

Growth Rates

Growth Rates(%)	Company	Industry	Sector	S&P 500
Sales (MRQ) vs Qtr. 1 Yr. Ago	135.99	16.76	17.44	16.55
Sales (TTM) vs TTM 1 Yr. Ago	128.98	9.03	10.33	16.56
Sales - 5 Yr. Growth Rate	-27.18	7.26	9.29	9.68
EPS (MRQ) vs Qtr. 1 Yr. Ago	101.70	27.42	22.40	18.14
EPS (TTM) vs TTM 1 Yr. Ago	99.99	16.75	17.75	20.27
EPS - 5 Yr. Growth Rate	-43.10	2.06	3.43	13.61
Capital Spending - 5 Yr. Growth Rate	-19.10	5.55	6.56	2.74

›Learn about Growth Rate Ratios

Financial Strength

Financial Strength	Company	Industry	Sector	S&P 500
Quick Ratio (MRQ)	0.85	0.52	0.50	1.22
Current Ratio (MRQ)	0.97	1.01	1.00	1.72
LT Debt to Equity (MRQ)	0.00	2.21	2.07	0.62
Total Debt to Equity (MRQ)	0.00	2.51	2.37	0.78
Interest Coverage (TTM)	NM	5.60	5.17	14.59

›Learn about Financial Condition Ratios

Profitability Ratios

Profitability Ratios (%)	Company	Industry	Sector	S&P 500
Gross Margin (TTM)	100.00	37.01	35.96	46.04
Gross Margin - 5 Yr. Avg.	100.00	32.00	32.67	45.13
EBITD Margin (TTM)	38.51	24.75	24.13	22.03
EBITD - 5 Yr. Avg.	38.32	26.86	26.06	20.01
Operating Margin (TTM)	30.29	15.84	15.47	20.66
Operating Margin - 5 Yr. Avg.	25.94	17.15	16.85	17.99
Pre-Tax Margin (TTM)	18.78	11.08	10.37	18.77
Pre-Tax Margin - 5 Yr. Avg.	10.12	10.95	11.20	16.62

	Company	Industry	Sector	S&P 500
Net Profit Margin (TTM)	15.36	7.97	8.25	13.68
Net Profit Margin - 5 Yr. Avg.	4.17	7.37	7.58	11.11
Effective Tax Rate (TTM)	18.21	31.06	30.90	30.78
Effective Tax Rate - 5 Yr. Avg.	29.91	33.75	33.48	33.09

›Learn about Profit Margin Ratios

Management Effectiveness

Management Effectiveness (%)	Company	Industry	Sector	S&P 500
Return On Assets (TTM)	3.49	2.85	3.08	7.86
Return On Assets - 5 Yr. Avg.	-0.03	2.54	2.64	6.27
Return On Investment (TTM)	4.03	3.36	3.74	11.83
Return On Investment - 5 Yr. Avg.	-0.23	3.11	3.25	9.92
Return On Equity (TTM)	11.63	15.67	14.77	19.92
Return On Equity - 5 Yr. Avg.	0.75	11.50	10.70	17.61

›Learn about Management Effectiveness

(http://www.investor.reuters.com/MG.aspx?ticker=IPR.N&target=/stocks/financialinfo/ratios/valuation)

GROWTH RATES

	1 Year	3 Years	5 Years
Sales %	-9.86	11.30	-27.18
EPS %	NM	52.17	-43.10
Dividend %	NM	NM	-100.00

›Learn about Growth Rate

REVENUE

Quarters	2002	2003	2004	2005
MAR	158	214	175	385
JUN	186	206	175	362
SEP	202	246	553	1,305
DEC	171	168	215	
Totals	717	834	1,118	2,052

Note: Units in Millions of British Pounds

›Learn about Revenue History

EARNINGS PER SHARE

Quarters	2002	2003	2004	2005
MAR	0.042	0.028	0.039	0.058
JUN	0.039	0.030	0.014	0.030
SEP	0.032	0.025	0.059	0.119
DEC	-0.020	-0.286	0.017	

Totals	0.093	-0.203	0.129	0.207

Note: Units in British Pounds

›Learn about EPS History

Consensus Estimates Analysis

In U.S. Dollars	# of Ests.	Mean Est.	High Est.	Low Est.	Std. Dev.	Proj. Pr/Est.
REVENUE (in Millions)						Pr/Sales
Quarter Ending Jun-05	-	-	-	-	-
Quarter Ending Sep-05	-	-	-	-	-
Year Ending Dec-05	1	3,213.00	3,213.00	3,213.00	0.00	19.08
Year Ending Dec-06	1	3,998.00	3,998.00	3,998.00	0.00	15.33
Earnings (per Share)						P/E
Quarter Ending Jun-05	-	-	-	-	-
Quarter Ending Sep-05	-	-	-	-	-
Year Ending Dec-05	2	2.30	2.31	2.28	0.01	18.11
Year Ending Dec-06	2	3.12	3.18	3.06	0.06	13.33
LT Growth Rate (%)	1	28.40	28.40	28.40	0.00	-

›Learn about EPS Estimates

(http://www.investor.reuters.com/CompanyFinancialHighlights.aspx?ticker=IPR.N&target=%2
fstocks%2ffinancialinfo%2fgrowth%2frate)

Efficiency				
Efficiency	Company	Industry	Sector	S&P 500
Revenue/Employee (TTM)	1,182,491	1,082,486	1,085,320	801,664
Net Income/Employee (TTM)	181,594	92,566	88,223	102,611
Receivable Turnover (TTM)	3.77	7.88	8.24	10.36
Inventory Turnover (TTM)	0.00	13.62	14.23	13.07
Asset Turnover (TTM)	0.23	0.39	0.43	0.98

›Learn about Efficiency Ratios

TOP FOREIGN UTILITIES COMPANIES BY MARKET CAP

Company	Symbol	Price	Change	Market Cap	P/E
Electricidade de Portugal SA (EDP)	EDP	28.19	+0.25%	102.68B	N/A
Scottish Power plc	SPI	36.85	-6.02%	68.67B	N/A
International Power plc	IPR	41.52	-0.74%	61.69B	217.38
Endesa SA	ELE	25.19	-0.75%	26.67B	14.39
TransCanada Corp.	TRP	30.37	+0.23%	14.79B	19.49
Empresa Nacional de Electricidad S.A.	EOC	30.00	-0.73%	8.20B	52.45

Showing 1 - 5 of 8 - View All

More Top Companies: by Performance, by Valuation, by Growth, more...

IPR VS. INDUSTRY LEADERS

Statistic	Industry Leader		IPR	IPR Rank
Market Capitalization	EDP	102.68B	61.69B	3 / 8
P/E Ratio (ttm)	IPR	217.38	-	1 / 8
PEG Ratio (ttm, 5 yr expected)	EDP	10.36	0.63	6 / 8
Revenue Growth (Qtrly YoY)	IPR	1.75%	-	1 / 8
EPS Growth (Qtrly YoY)	IPR	2.09%	-	1 / 8
Long-Term Growth Rate (5 yr)	ENI	33.6%	28.4%	2 / 8
Return on Equity (ttm)	ELE	16.33%	8.84%	4 / 8
Long-Term Debt/Equity (mrq)	EDP	2.363	1.928	2 / 8
Dividend Yield (annual)	IPR	7.70%	-	1 / 8

(http://finance.yahoo.com/q/in?s=IPR)

In the above mentioned ratios, International Power is the leader in Revenue Growth, Earnings per share growth Price Earnings ratio and dividend yield ratio. It has the second in long term growth rate and the third best in market capitalisation, indicating that the company is not only in good financial position but it is using its resources effectively for success in the long term. The company also provides good return on equity, which indicates that the shareholders are confident of a good dividend and also of the price of the stock when they want to sell in the long term. I would buy this stock as a long term investment and not as a speculative investment.

MARKET CAPITALISATION:

Leaders in Market Capitalization

EDP ELEC DE PORT SA [EDP]	**$101.7 B**
SCOTTISH PWR ADS [SPI]	**$72.8 B**
INTERNATIONAL POWER [IPR]	**$62.3 B**
ENDESA SA ADS [ELE]	**$26.7 B**
TRANSCANADA CORP [TRP]	**$14.7 B**
EMPRESA NATL ELECTRI [EOC]	**$8.3 B**
ENERSIS S A [ENI]	**$7.7 B**
CONS WATER CO INC [CWCO]	**$222.4 M**

Laggards in Market Capitalization

CONS WATER CO INC [CWCO]	**$222.4 M**
ENERSIS S A [ENI]	**$7.7 B**
EMPRESA NATL ELECTRI [EOC]	**$8.3 B**
TRANSCANADA CORP [TRP]	**$14.7 B**
ENDESA SA ADS [ELE]	**$26.7 B**
INTERNATIONAL POWER [IPR]	**$62.3 B**
SCOTTISH PWR ADS [SPI]	**$72.8 B**
EDP ELEC DE PORT SA [EDP]	**$101.7 B**

(http://biz.yahoo.com/ic/ll/910mkt.html)

INDUSTRY STATISTICS:

Industry Statistics

Market Capitalization:	294B
Price / Earnings:	15.5
Price / Book:	2.0
Net Profit Margin (mrq):	7.2%
Price To Free Cash Flow (mrq):	-359.4
Return on Equity:	11.5%
Total Debt / Equity:	0.0
Dividend Yield:	4.7%

International Power Plc ADR (IPR)

Current P/E: 18.3

Nov 23 12:03am ET †

Analist consensus recommendation: 1.3

1.0 - 1.5: Strong Buy   **1.6 - 2.5**: Buy   **2.6 - 3.5**: Hold   **3.6 - 4.5**: Underperform   **4.6 - 5.0**: Sell

	Qtr Sep/2005	Qtr Dec/2005	FY Dec/2005	FY Dec/2006
Current Mean EPS	NA	NA	2.30	3.12
Number of Brokers	0	0	2	2
Year-Ago EPS	NA	NA	0.13	2.30
Current High	NA	NA	2.31	3.18
Current Low	NA	NA	2.28	3.06
Median	NA	NA	2.30	3.12

Standard Deviation	NA	NA	0.02	0.08
Current vs. Year-Ago	NA	NA	1669%	35%
Report Date	03-Nov-2005	07-Mar-2006		

Reported Quarters

	Last Qtr	2 Qtrs Ago	3 Qtrs Ago	4 Qtrs Ago
Previous Estimate	NA	NA	NA	NA
Previous Actual EPS				

Earnings Estimate Revisions and Trends

	Qtr Sep/2005	Qtr Dec/2005	FY Dec/2005	FY Dec/2006
Current Mean	NA	NA	2.30	3.12
7-Days Ago Mean	NA	NA		
30-Days Ago Mean	NA	NA		
60-Days Ago Mean	NA	NA		
90-Days Ago Mean	NA	NA		
Up Revisions Last 7 Days	0	0	0	1
Up Revisions Last 30 Days	0	0	0	1
Down Revisions Last 7 Days	0	0	0	1
Down Revisions Last 30 Days	0	0	2	1

Consensus Recommendations		Long Term Growth Rates	
Current Mean	1.3	Next 5 Years - Median	28.4
Number of Brokers	3	Number of Brokers	1
Industry Mean		Industry Growth Rate	

7-Days Ago Mean	1.0	Next 5 Years High		28.4
30-Days Ago Mean	1.0	Next 5 Years Low		28.4
60-Days Ago Mean	1.0	Last 5 Years Actual		-2.5
90-Days Ago Mean	1.0			
Sector Mean				
WSJ/DJ US Mean	2.46			

Comparative Estimates and Trends

	Sep/2005	Dec/2005	CY 2005	CY 2006
Company	NA	NA	2.30	3.12
Current vs. Year-Ago Change	NA	NA	1669%	35%
Industry -				
Current vs. Year-Ago Change	NA	NA	NA	NA
Sector -				
Current vs. Year-Ago Change	NA	NA	NA	NA
WSJ/DJ US - Universe	4.68	4.71	17.38	20.05
Current vs. Year-Ago Change	16%	15%	15%	15%

Ratios relative to:	Company	Industry	Sector	WSJ/DJ US
P/E on Calendar Year Mean	18.3			17.11
PEG on Calendar Year Mean	0.64			1.58

(http://www.money.cnn.com/earnings/profiles/IPR.html)

International Pwr Plc (NYSE)   Chart Financial Analyst Insider Msg News Option

IPR   **42.45**   **+0.85**   **+2.04%**   Vol: 3,500   1:14pm 11/23/05

	This Quarter	Next Quarter	This Fiscal	Next Fiscal
# of Estimates			2.00	2.00
Mean Estimate			2.30	3.12
High Estimates			2.31	3.18
Low Estimates			2.28	3.06
Coefficient Variance			0.92	2.72

IBES data provided by Thomson Financial Solutions

LIMITATIONS OF THE DATA PUBLISHED IN THE ACCOUNTS AND REPORTS:

The data published in the balance sheet at the end of the year and the Income Statement for the year ended records the transactions for that particular year. T   he data is not sufficient to analyse the future performance of the company as there are many other factors that have to be taken into account like the changes in the economy, the market, the government regulations etc. However, all other factors remaining more or less constant, the annual accounts of the company do provide a good indication of the performance of the company in the future. However, the company does not perform consistently every year, there are always factors affecting the performance of the company. Hence any future forecasts are only estimates. Even the Random Walk theory states that the share price of the company does not follow a consistent pattern. The markets are highly volatile.

The ratio analysis and other predictions are based on the information provided in the Balance Sheet and the Profit and Loss Account by the company. There are certain items like depreciation and contingent liabilities etc. that are included in the statements of accounts which are calculated according to the company policy in accordance with the laws of the country in which the company is situated. Such figures are only estimates and hence the assets may be overvalued or undervalued. Certain items may be wrongly capitalized, while other items may be wrongly treated as revenue. Sometimes in cases of fixed assets, the values given in the Balance Sheet may not be a good indicator of the real value of the asset as there may be more or less depreciation charged in that particular year, although the company may have adhered strictly with all laws.

International Power operates in both US and the UK, and has to follow both USGAAP and UKGAAP. The calculations in both significantly differ giving different figures for both the US and UK authorities and the investors. Disclosure requirements under both the systems are also different.

International Power, Mitsui to Buy Calpine U.K. Plant (Update4)

May 31 (Bloomberg) -- International Power Plc, an electricity producer on four continents, and Japanese trading company Mitsui & Co. will pay U.S.-based Calpine Corp. 490 million pounds ($889 million) for its Saltend plant in the U.K.

International Power will have a 70 percent stake and Mitsui 30 percent in the 1,200-megawatt Saltend Energy Centre, Mitsui said today in a statement to the Tokyo Stock Exchange. Calpine, which owns power plants in 21 states, put its largest generator up for sale in January.

London-based International Power is adding the plant to its portfolio after U.K. power prices recovered, soaring 49 percent in the past 12 months. Mitsui President Shoei Utsuda is investing in overseas power assets to help maintain earnings growth at the Tokyo-based trader and double its generating capacity to 6,000 megawatts by 2010.

``Mitsui and other Japanese trading companies are looking for a wide range of projects to spread risk as they aggressively grow their power plant business in the next four to five years,'' Shuichi Hirukawa, an analyst at Meiji Dresdner Asset Management Co. in Tokyo, said in a telephone interview today. Meiji Dresdner managed the equivalent of $11.6 billion in assets as of September 2004. ``There seem to be many opportunities.''

In December, International Power and Mitsui completed a $2 billion purchase of stakes in 10 power plants owned by Edison International in Europe, Australia, Indonesia and Puerto Rico. They have a total capacity of 4,666 megawatts. The two companies also have run projects together in Pakistan and Abu Dhabi.

Shares of Mitsui rose 12 yen, or 1.3 percent, to close at 975 on the Tokyo Stock exchange. Earlier today the shares gained as much as 2 percent to 982 yen.

Calpine's Debt

Calpine plans to sell off power plants to pare its $18 billion in debt by $3 billion this year. The company's stock last month dropped to a record low, and prices for its bonds tumbled to below 50 cents on the dollar amid concern creditors might force Calpine into bankruptcy.

The company plans to cut annual operating costs by about $200 million, partly by closing plants in regions where power markets are depressed.

Calpine agreed to buy Saltend, a gas-fired plant near Hull in the north of England, in July 2001 for about $800 million from Entergy Corp. The plant, a supplier to the nearby BP Plc chemicals factory and to the wholesale power market, can generate enough to light 1.2 million homes.

International Power will pay 150 million pounds for a 70 percent stake in Saltend and Mitsui 65 million pounds for 30 percent, the statement said. Five commercial banks in Europe will finance the rest, a Mitsui spokesman said, declining to give details.

U.K. Power Prices

U.K. power prices have recovered from a 40 percent plunge between 1998 and 2002, following the industry's opening up to competition. Low prices bankrupted the country's largest power company, British Energy Group Plc, and threatened the same to its largest power station, Drax. Drax Group Ltd., owner of the Drax power station, is now preparing for a stock market listing at the end of the year.

U.K. power prices for next month's delivery have soared in the past year, following an increase in natural gas and oil prices. The rise has attracted traders to the market.

Cargill Inc., the world's largest agricultural company, said on Jan. 21 it started trading U.K. electricity and gas in London, expanding its Geneva-based European business.

Scottish Power Plc, the U.K.'s fifth-largest energy provider, bought the Damhead Creek and Brighton power stations last year. Scottish & Southern Energy Plc, the country's fourth-largest energy supplier, bought two coal-fired stations, Fiddler's Ferry and Ferrybridge, also last year.

To contact the reporter on this story:

Meggan Richard in Tokyo at mrichard3@bloomberg.net;

Hector Forster in Tokyo at hforster@bloomberg.net.

International Power plc Completes Sale Of Interest In 300 MW Valley Power plant

2005 Oct 17 6:00 AM

International Power plc and Mitsui & Co, Ltd announced that they have completed the sale of 60% interest in the 300 MW Valley Power peaking plant in Victoria, Australia, to Snowy Hydro Ltd

International Power plc Completes Acquisition Of 1,200 MW Saltend Power Plant

2005 Jul 28 6:17 PM

International Power plc announced that it has completed the acquisition of the 1,200 MW CCGT Saltend Power Plant in Hull, England in a 70:30 partnership with Mitsui & Co., Ltd of Japan. Saltend was acquired from Calpine Corporation for a total consideration of £500 million. The total consideration includes the valuation of the plant and the associated gas and power contracts, and the acquisition will be funded by a mix of debt and equity in a 55:45 ratio.

International Power plc Secures $640 Million Credit Facility

2005 Jun 8 4:00 AM

International Power plc announced that it has signed a new $640 million (£352 million) corporate Revolving Credit Facility with its core relationship banks which will run until October 2008, with an option to extend for a maximum of two years subject to lenders' consent. The new facility replaces the existing $450 million (£247 million) facility, which was due to expire in October 2006. The Mandated Lead Arrangers for this facility were ABN AMRO Bank N.V., Calyon, ING Bank N.V., and The Royal Bank of Scotland plc.

.(http://today.reuteurs.com/stock/keydevelopments/aspx?ticker=IPR.N)

REFERENCES:

1)http://today.reuteurs.com/stock/keydevelopments/aspx?ticker=IPR.N
2)IBES data provided by Thomson Financial Solutions
3)http;//www.money.cnn.com/earnings/profiles/IPR.html
4)http://biz.yahoo.com/ic/ll/910mkt.html
5)http://finance.yahoo.com/q/in?s=IPR
6)
http://www.investor.reuters.com/CompanyFinancialHighlights.aspx?ticker=IPR.N&target=%2fst
ocks%2ffinancialinfo%2fgrowth%2frate

7)
http://www.investor.reuters.com/MG.aspx?ticker=IPR.N&target=/stocks/financialinfo/ratios/valuation

8)http://finance.yahoo.com

9)http://briefing.com

10)http://mwprices.ft.com

11)http://www.hoovers.com/international-power/--ID__47995,ticker__--/free-co-fin-factsheet.xht

12)http://money.cnn.com

13)http://www.biz.yahoo.com/ic/47/47995.87

14)http://www.bloomberg.com

15)Pego, Tejo Energia Portugal(2003)(13)

16)http://www.investis.com/ip/reports/ar2004/content/operating

17)http://www.investor.reuters.com

18)Annual Report for 2003 of International Power, Pgs. 1-4, 11

www.ingramcontent.com/pod-product-compliance
Lightning Source LLC
Chambersburg PA
CBHW051700170526
45167CB00002B/472